# PANCHO VILLA
# AND THE MEXICAN REVOLUTION

## INTERLINK ILLUSTRATED HISTORIES

# PANCHO VILLA

## AND THE MEXICAN REVOLUTION

### MANUEL PLANA

Translated by Arthur Figliola

## INTERLINK BOOKS

An imprint of Interlink Publishing Group, Inc.

New York • Northampton

First American edition published in 2002 by

**INTERLINK BOOKS**
An imprint of Interlink Publishing Group, Inc.
99 Seventh Avenue · Brooklyn, New York 11215 and
46 Crosby Street · Northampton, Massachusetts 01060

Copyright © Giunti Gruppo Editoriale — Casterman
Translation copyright © Interlink Publishing 2002

This edition of *Pancho Villa and the Mexican Revolution* is published
by arrangement with Giunti Gruppo Editoriale and Casterman Editions.

**Library of Congress Cataloging-in-Publication Data**
Plana, Manuel.
[Pancho Villa e la Rivoluzione messicana. English]
Pancho Villa and the Mexican Revolution / by Marco Palla ; translated
by Arthur Figliola.– 1st American ed.
  p. cm.
Includes bibliographical references.
ISBN 1-56656-401-8
1. Villa, Pancho, 1878-1923. 2. Mexico–History–1910-1946. I.
Title.
F1234.V63 P54 2001
972.08'16–dc21

                                    2001003656

On the cover: Pancho Villa and Emiliano Zapata on December 6, 1914, the day of their triumphal entry
into Mexico City.

Unless otherwise indicated, the images in this volume are taken from the Giunti Iconographic Archives.
Giunti Gruppo Editoriale declares itself fully prepared to settle claims regarding those images for which
the original proprietor has been impossible to locate.

Typeset by Archetype IT Ltd., website: www.archetype-it.com
Printed and bound in Italy

To order or request our complete catalog,
please call us at **1-800-238-LINK** or write to:
**Interlink Publishing**
46 Crosby Street, Northampton, MA 01060
e-mail: interpg@aol.com • website: www.interlinkbooks.com

# Contents

# PANCHO VILLA
# AND THE MEXICAN REVOLUTION

# Chapter 1

# **M**EXICO **B**EFORE
# THE **R**EVOLUTION

AT THE END OF THE LAST CENTURY, MEXICO'S ECONOMY GREW REMARKABLY – BUT SO DID THE COUNTRY'S SOCIAL INEQUALITY. PROTESTS BY THE URBAN MIDDLE CLASS AND THE FARMERS' MOVEMENT BROKE DOWN ANCIENT STRUCTURES OF DOMINATION, CLEARING THE WAY FOR A REVOLUTION THAT WOULD BREAK OUT IN 1910, AND LAST FOR A DECADE.

I n 1910, Mexico had a population of 15 million, and occupied a territory of about 772,000 square miles. The population was overwhelmingly rural, concentrated in the central plateau. This region – the heartland of pre-Hispanic Mexico – constituted the choice area for human habitation, given its favorable geographic and climatic conditions. The agricultural workforce in the *haciendas*, the large rural landholdings, numbered 3fi million. Slightly more than 100,000 people were employed in mining, and approximately 500,000 in various sectors of industry and transportation. The populations of only four cities exceeded 50,000; the capital, Mexico City, had a population of about a half million.

In the last decades of the nineteenth century, Mexico, along with other nations, made important material progress by virtue of extremely close and established ties with the modern industrial and imperialist powers. Several regions of the country began to concentrate on new commercial crops, such as coffee, cotton, and *henequén*, a fiber used in the manufacture of bags and cord. In the north, ranching expanded. Statutory changes permitting the sale at low cost of uncultivated terrain and ancient communal lands increased large-landholding. These large

*In the period following independence in 1821, Mexican history was characterized by many attempts to give the country stability. Conflicts between liberals and conservatives marked the life of the nation during the mid-nineteenth century. At left, the municipal palace of Monterrey at the turn of the century.*

*The hacienda was the principal institution of the rural world. With dimensions that often reached tens of thousands of acres, it was the economic base of the social and political power of the landowning class. Below, the hacienda Xcanchakan in the region of Yucatan, in an 1860 photo.*

landowners created new haciendas, from which they extracted substantial economic gain, while at the same time impeding the growth of a class of smaller-scale farmers.

In indigenous lands, the farmers lost much of their common land and were forced to depend on the haciendas for work, for which they were paid a quantity of corn or grain barely sufficient to guarantee sustenance.

After 1880, the discovery in the north of minerals that would serve as raw materials for the industrialized powers led to the development of a modern mining industry. The same time saw the introduction of a rail network that, by the end of the nineteenth century, was about 12,500 miles in length. The railroads facilitated communications and encouraged economic integration between distant regions of the country. Modern textile factories were constructed and mercantile activities developed. Foreign capital-

ists – especially from the United States and England – invested in mines, railroads, electricity, and oil, one of Mexico's more plentiful natural resources. The commercial and financial sectors of the economy attracted the attention of German and, to a lesser extent, French entrepreneurs.

By the century's end, these new trends and developments were especially concentrated in the north, where mines, foundries, railroads, modern agriculture, livestock production, commerce, and banking developed faster than elsewhere. The United States, with its powerful industrial economy and geographic proximity, especially benefited from Mexico's economic expansion, and American capitalists quickly prevailed over their European counterparts – something that became even more pronounced as World War I began.

Discontent in the countryside and the social unease generated by rapid and inequitable economic growth

helped spark the 1910 Revolution, but the immediate cause must be seen in the context of a national political crisis whose roots lay deeper in the history of Mexico.

### The Liberals and the Conservative Reaction

In 1821, Mexico won its independence after eleven years of acute internal conflicts and war against Spain. In 1824, a constitution establishing the republican and federal systems was ratified, but subsequent governments were weak. The temporal power of the Church, which was stronger and had a broader influence in Mexico than in other nations in the Americas, remained intact, and Spaniards continued to hold important positions in the government, the army, and the ecclesiastical hierarchy. In fact, despite official independence, a conservative mood prevailed for the first half of the century.

*Day workers, who generally lived in miserable conditions, were the main work force on the country's large properties.*

During this period, Mexico suffered a series of external threats that weakened its governments and drained its limited financial resources. In 1829, Spain attempted an invasion; in 1836, Texas became independent; and in 1848, war with the United States ended with the loss of California and New Mexico.

The liberal revolution of 1855 signaled a clear fracture within Mexican political life. The liberals tried to defeat the strong conservative bloc, create a modern administration, and promote economic progress. In 1856, the government passed its first law regulating the sale of ecclesiastical properties, in order to secure new fiscal income, divide up privately owned property, and limit the power of the church. The constitution of 1857 sanctioned the nationalization of church property, and in fact most of it was taken away until 1863. For the first time in Mexican history, the constitution introduced articles about individuals' rights. It reinstated the federal system, which had been suppressed by the conservatives, conceded substantial

## MEXICO ON THE EVE OF REVOLUTION

Lost in 1836
Ceded in 1848
Ceded in 1853

0     miles     620

San Francisco

CALIFORNIA

Salt Lake City

UTAH

Los Angeles

Colorado

ARIZONA

Phoenix

Tucson

Santa Fe

TEXAS

Río Grande

Chihuahua

GULF OF MEXICO

M E X I C O

PACIFIC

Zacatecas

Celaya

Mérida

YUCATAN

Guadalupe-Hidalgo

Mexico City

Veracruz

OCEAN

Tegucigalpa

Guatemala

politico-administrative and fiscal prerogatives to the governments and legislative assemblies of the single states, and in sum, fixed the principles of a secular and reform-oriented society.

But in 1858, the conservative and Church reaction to these reforms gave birth to a civil war that lasted three years and prolonged itself with an attempt to install a monarchy under the protection of a European power. With military and financial support from Napoleon III's France, which was following imperialist aims of its own, the Austrian Maximilian was installed as emperor. He arrived in Mexico in May 1864, accompanied by his wife, Princess Charlotte of Belgium. The imperial government, however, proved to be incapable of maintaining the nation's course, and the emperor's reign lasted only three years. Without the support of the French, Maximilian was defeated by the

*With the Treaty of Guadalupe Hidalgo, which concluded the war against the United States (1846–1848) and established the border on the Río Grande, Mexico lost California and New Mexico; the secession of Texas had occurred during the preceding decade.*

*The Mexican adventure of Archduke Maximilian of Hapsburg concluded tragically in 1867. Napoleon III's dream of an empire on the other side of the Atlantic collapsed. Above, the execution of Maximilian, rendered by Edouard Manet between 1867 and 1868.*

armed resistance of the liberals. During their withdrawal from Mexico, the French also faced diplomatic pressure from the United States, which, at the end of its own Civil War, began to enforce the principle that European powers should not interfere in the internal affairs of nations in the Western hemisphere.

### The Age of Porfirio Díaz

The restoration of the republican regime in 1867, under the guidance of Benito Juárez, a central figure of the liberal period in Mexico, opened a difficult phase of political reform that lasted for a decade, and ended with the entry of new leaders on the political scene.

Porfirio Díaz's rise to power in 1877 signaled a break from the liberal and reform culture of the preceding period, and inaugurated a 30-year conservative regime that, in practice, became a personal dictatorship. In 1887, the constitution was modified to provide for the re-election of the sitting president, and from that time, Díaz was re-installed at the expiration of each of his mandates. This provision was extended to the governors of the single states, in an attempt to stabilize local governments, and effectively, more and more Díaz was able to approve the candidates himself. The political system, in this way, became the prerogative of a small elite which, over a period of over 30 years, counted scarcely more than 50 people among its ministerial charges, and fewer than 200 among state governors.

The regime of Porfirio Díaz (1877–1911) offered many opportunities to foreign capitalists, conceding enormous expanses of uncultivated lands to large landowners and foreign investors. Díaz, in the name of progress, strongly supported the various dominant regional groups; in this way, the local elites strengthened their hold on economic and political power. In 1910, the final re-election campaign for Díaz, who was at that point in his 80s, created a grave internal crisis, arousing both social and political tensions. The events that followed led to his fall a few months later, and to the rise of armed move-

## BENITO JUÁREZ: THE LIBERAL REFORMS

**B**orn in 1806, in Guelatao, Oaxaca to an indigenous family of farmers, Benito Juárez completed his study of law in Oaxaca. In January 1856, he became governor of the state, and by the end of the following year, vice president of the republic. The conservatives reacted negatively to the liberal constitution approved in 1857, and president Ignacio Comonfort, after some hesitation, tendered his resignation and went into exile. Juárez, who succeeded him as president in May 1858, established his government in Veracruz; he started a civil war that concluded on January 1, 1861, with a Liberal victory. The serious financial difficulties of the moment persuaded Juárez, in mid-July, 1861, to ask Congress to suspend foreign debt repayments for a period of two years. Shortly after this announcement, England and France broke off diplomatic relations with Mexico. At the beginning of 1862, the naval forces of these two European powers joined with those of Spain in a landing at Veracruz. An understanding was reached with England and Spain. The French, allied with the Mexican conservatives, opened hostilities, intending to march on the capital, which they entered in June 1863, installing the imperial government of Maximilian of Hapsburg. Juárez retreated to El Paso del Norte — which in 1888 changed its name, in his honor, to Ciudad Juárez — and organized the resistance against the foreign occupiers. The foreigners were defeated on May 15, 1867, at Querétaro; Maximilian, commanding the imperial troops, was arrested, tried, and, on June 19, executed before a firing squad. Juárez re-established republican order, and was confirmed president. He died on July 19, 1872. ■

ments and new social groups that changed the political reality of the country.

### The Leaders of the Revolution

The Mexican Revolution of 1910 came about, like most, because a majority of the population had suffered rather than benefited from the economic "progress" and prosperity of the Porfirian years. But in the case of this revolution, the absence of modern political parties or a worker's movement capable of guiding the revolts of the rural and urban masses transformed the popular bosses into national leaders and the struggle's protagonists. The revolutionaries, who belonged to different social classes, were in large measure men of northern Mexico. One of the most

*Ciudad Juárez, on the border with the United States, was one of the urban centers that registered notable economic progress at the turn of the century.*

important among these was Francisco Madero, the principal opponent of Porfirio Díaz in the presidential elections of 1910, and a member of a wealthy Nuevo León family, whose industrial and financial activities were at the center of a vast network of interests.

Venustiano Carranza, in contrast, was a farmer from the state of Coahuila, and one of the few revolutionary leaders with active political experience in the Porfirian administration. Alvaro Obregón came from a family of small farmers from the southern Sonora. By 1914, many local leaders were able to mobilize various regions of the center and south.

Pancho Villa, the quintessential popular revolutionary hero, was originally from the northern state of Durango, but spent many years in the southern half of neighboring Chihuahua. Many popular leaders came from these two regions. The only exception of note is Emiliano Zapata, who was active in the small central state of Morelos; other exceptions were the minor heads of the rural districts surrounding Mexico City.

The revolutionary decade beginning in 1910 may be divided into three phases. The first was characterized by the coming to power of Francisco Madero (1911–1913), who was deposed in a coup by General Victoriano Huerta in February 1913. The second phase, distinct from the attempt to overthrow the counter-revolutionary government, ended in the revolutionary civil war of 1914–1915. The final period culminated in the ratification of the constitution of 1917 and the ascendance of Venustiano Carranza to the presidency (1917–1920).

### The Immense Territories of the North

From the very start, the northern state of Chihuahua was Pancho Villa's power base. In a sense, Pancho Villa's star rose with Chihuahua's, for with its natural resources and proximity to the United States, Chihuahua began to exert substantial influence over all of northern Mexico, as well as the rest of the nation.

*In the northern regions of the country, the exploitation of mineral resources contributed to the growth of the regional economy.*

*Above,* Work in the Mines, *a fresco by Diego Rivera, in the Department of Public Education in Mexico City.*

Villa quickly proved capable of successfully mobilizing diverse social classes. Beginning in 1913, in fact, he became one of the principal protagonists of the revolution, and, using his control of the Chihuahuan state as a base, he successfully dominated truly vast territories for a number of years, though he reached the apex of his political and military power in the years surrounding the revolution.

Comprising approximately 153,000 square miles (about half the size of France), Chihuahua is the largest state in the Mexican federation. Its population in 1910 was nearly 400,000, concentrated in the

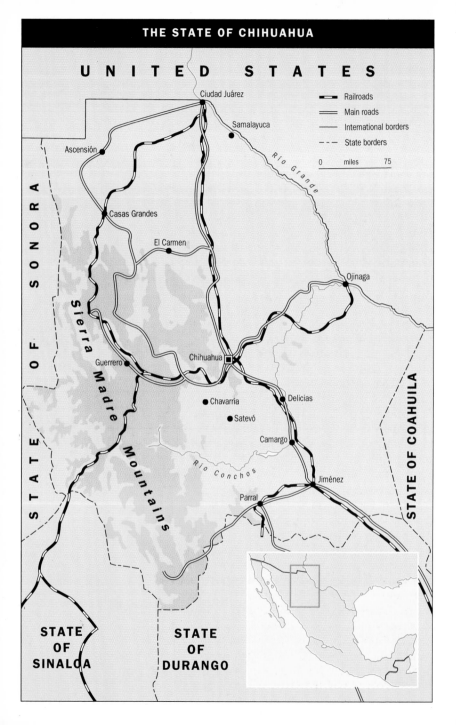

# THE STATE OF CHIHUAHUA

UNITED STATES

Railroads
Main roads
International borders
State borders

0        miles        75

Ciudad Juárez
Samalayuca
Ascensión
Rio Grande
Casas Grandes
El Carmen
Ojinaga
Sierra Madre Mountains
Guerrero
Chihuahua
Chavarría
Satevó
Delicias
Camargo
Rio Conchos
Jiménez
Parral

STATE OF SONORA

STATE OF COAHUILA

STATE OF SINALOA

STATE OF DURANGO

three principal cities of Ciudad Juárez (on the border with Texas, 230 miles from the state capital), Chihuahua (930 miles from Mexico City), and Parral, farther to the south. Additional population centers in Chihuahua include about 60 municipalities spread along the slopes of the western cordillera and valleys of the southern rivers that flow into the Río Conchos, a principal artery of the eastern plains and tributary of the Río Grande.

The other regions bordering on the United States (Baja California, Sonora, Coahuila, and Tamaulipas) and others constituting the "north" (Tepic or Nayarit, Sinaloa, Durango, Nuevo León, San Luis Potosí, and Zacatecas) have, like Chihuahua, enormous territorial expanses and sparse populations. In the last decades of the nineteenth century, the economies of these territories expanded rapidly following their link-up with the US rail network and the further development of extractive industries, livestock production, and export-dependent agricultural production.

*Bordering on the United States and comprising over 150,000 square miles, Chihuahua is Mexico's largest state. Sparsely populated, with few population centers spread over a vast territory, the region's development was tied to copper, lead, and zinc mining, as well as cattle breeding.*

During the colonial period, the Chihuahuan economy was based on the extraction of precious metals in the south, around Parral; in the remaining semi-arid lands of the region, livestock production predominated. The discovery in the mid-sixteenth century of silver veins in the Zacatecas Mountains had opened the way for the colonization of the vast northern territories. Urban centers and agricultural settlements grew up around the mining activity, and the many local indigenous groups, many semi-nomadic, were forced to succumb to the colonizers. Only a few groups, primarily those located along the western cordillera, were able to preserve their own ways of life.

The establishment of Anglo-American colonies in Texas in the second decade of the nineteenth century, as well as the march westward after the 1848 discovery of gold in California, forced the Indians of the territories beyond the Río Grande to move into unoccupied spaces, ever closer to the border with Mexico. The Apaches, who had always constituted a human barrier in the northern Sonora, began to pour back into the state of Chihuahua in search of land as the rail networks of the American southwest slowly

*Mines and railroads – the basis of much of Mexico's economic growth during the regime of Porfirio Díaz, 1877–1911.*

expanded. This gave rise to a costly and cruel campaign – by the authorities, the landowners, and the livestock interests of the region – to exterminate them.

In northern Mexico, the settlements became concentrated around the few military camps and in fertile areas around population centers, which, with the passage of time, gained dominance over old communal lands. The frontiersmen who populated these new settlements were exposed to continual insecurity and grew accustomed to their distance from the political center of the nation. In this way, the famously rough, individualistic character of the frontiersman emerged. The settlements were without signs of the ethnic mixing typical of regions to the south.

To this day, economic activity in the north remains tied to precious metal industries. In 1880, when rail construction brought an end to the north's isolation with links between central Mexico and various points on the US rail network, it lay the groundwork for the development of new economic activities. The first railroad in Mexico, financed by English interests and opened in 1873, united the capital with the port city of Veracruz, on the Gulf of Mexico. The most impor-

tant lines expanded gradually, with secondary and intermediate branches. Mostly built by financiers from the United States, these lines initiated at points bordering on the United States (Ciudad Juárez, Piedras Negras, and Nuevo Laredo) and eventually converged near the center and capital.

### The Peculiarities of Chihuahua

After 1880, the discovery of new mineral resources in the north generated important and complementary commercial activities. Sonora, Chihuahua, and Durango become the nation's principal producers of copper, lead, and zinc, to the partial detriment of

the traditional mining regions in the central states, as well as to silver production in general. The concessions framework already in force in the mining industry brought great wealth to very few hands, such as US-born William C. Greene in Cananea, northern Sonora, or the few foreign companies that mined coal near the Sabinas River, in the state of Coahuila. The American Smelting and Refining company, after merging with the Guggenheims in 1901, exercised a virtual

## THE NORTH: CONSEQUENCES OF ECONOMIC GROWTH

The Mexican north grew significantly during Porfirio Díaz's 30-year rule – economic growth that altered the region's social structure. Mexican scholars still debate the significance of the revolution of 1910 in this matter. Héctor Aguilar Camín, historian and journalist, stresses the importance of the revolution in completing the north's integration with the rest of the country.

"Modernity came to the north with the railroads, US investments, intensive agriculture, the extraction of industrial metals, and commerce in ports. In the north, the obstacles typical of ancient Mexico – its ethnic and regional diversity – were largely absent, as were the weight of religious and Hispanic traditions, and reactionary agrarian struggles that the liberal project had wanted to abolish in order to create a secularized and capitalist Mexico. It is significant that this same north, once so open to changes requested by the liberals, decided in 1910 to dominate the nation by means of the same railroad lines that once united it. This strategy would continue for the next 25 years. The prevailing image of the revolution is that its heart lay in the Zapatista agrarian movement. Perhaps its true significance is revealed in the opposite hypothesis: the armies of the north brought to power the children of an immense region that had no shared historical or human connection with the center or south." ■

From: Héctor Aguilar Camín, *Saldos de la Revolución* (Mexico City: Ediciones Océano, 1984) 12–3.

monopoly over the Mexican mining industry, with foundries in Monterrey, Aguascalientes, Chihuahua, and Velardena, in Durango.

At the end of the century, the city of Chihuahua became an important center of mercantile interests for the entire northern mining region. These interests were controlled in large measure by US merchants, to the detriment of the local middle classes: in fact, foreign residents numbered about 5,000 in a population of 39,000. In other industrial cities such as Monterrey, Saltillo, and Torreón, the presence of foreign merchants was also quite marked, though perhaps less so than in Chihuahua.

As these facts would suggest, the records of land ownership during the last decades of the nineteenth century also reveal a rapid process of concentration in the hands of a few, changing the shape of the ruling regional classes.

*The young Porfirio Díaz played a role of great importance in the war undertaken by the liberals to rid the country of French invasion forces commanded by the Count de Lorencez.*

## PORFIRIO DIAZ: A 30-YEAR REGIME

**B**orn in 1830 in Oaxaca to a family of humble origins, Díaz became active in the ranks of the liberal movement, participating in the Battle of Puebla (fought on May 5, 1862 against the French), and on April 2, 1867, led the re-conquest of the city against the supporters of Maximilian. Strengthened by his newly found prestige, Díaz asserted himself during the presidential election with the help of the moderate liberals in 1871 and 1875. He became president in 1877. After the presidential interlude of Manuel Gonzalez (1880–1884), Díaz was re-elected again and again until he was removed from power in 1911, by the opposition led

by Francesco Madero. He found exile in Europe, where he died in Paris in 1915. Mexican historian Daniel Cosío Villegas, who has specialized in the study of the Díaz regime, offered this succinct portrait of Díaz's political personality: "Despite Porfirio's and his

supporters' self-characterizations as liberals and reformists, no-one was fooled by the fact that they represented something else: but what? Porfirio, himself, could not fill in this lacuna since, excepting the clear notion of authority that a government must possess and demand, as well as his declared penchant for control and order, he had nothing to fill it with. From his circle, or cabinet, he received little assistance.... The difficulties with which Díaz had to struggle were multiple and serious, and the personal resources of his group very limited." ■

From: Daniel Cosío Villegas, *Llamadas* (Mexico City: El Colegio de Mexico, 1980) 221.

The colonization laws of 1884 conceded enormous expanses of uncultivated land, and the sale of communally owned lands began. This phenomenon, which took on national dimensions, fomented rural revolts. In Chihuahua, for example, the indigenous Tarahumara of the cordillera lost their lands, which surrounded the military camps and settlements of the northern districts. These were lands they had been counting on to lease to, or otherwise derive profit from, forestry and mining concerns (some American-owned) and large-scale livestock breeders. The series of rural revolts provoked by these initiatives was repressed by the federal army.

On the eve of the revolution, Chihuahua was the keystone of the economic empire of Luis Terrazas, who has made of this state a true family fiefdom. Underlying his fortune was an immense landholding covering nearly six million acres of the state's fertile lands. His land had been subdivided into several cattle-breeding haciendas that, together, claimed over 400,000 head. By marrying their fourteen children to the principal families of the region, the Terrazas clan came to dominate the economy and politics of the state. One of the clan's members, Enrique Creel – the son of an ex-American consul and son-in-law of Luis Terrazas – was elected state governor in 1904, and became the key figure in the family's negotiations with foreign mining interests in Chihuahua. He was also influential in finances at the national level.

The control of the Minero Bank of Chihuahua, founded in 1882, and of other local institutions, insured the Terraza family dominance over regional credit, and allowed them to broaden their financial dealings with other northern industrial groups. These in turn owned the textile factories of the provincial capital, a large number of the manufacturing enterprises, including meat production, grain mills, and the only plant for beer manufacture, and also developable tracts of land in the capital. The Terrazas were also the owners of public transport lines in the

*The conditions of the popular classes and marginalized members of society led to the revolution that brought down the Díaz regime.*

*At the end of the nineteenth century, in the northern mining regions, a wave of strikes organized by workers to improve living conditions eroded the stability of the Díaz regime.*

three principal cities, as well as the telephone and telegraph company. They also eventually acquired numerous mining concessions, which were later contracted to US companies.

The dominant class during the regime of Porfirio Díaz generally invested, as did the Terrazas, in several sectors of the economy, but the status of the regional oligarchies differed. Others may have invested in industry and finance, but no other local elite could boast a political, economic, and territorial domination as vast as the Terrazas', with such financial autonomy, with such solid national presence, with such strong ties to foreign capitalists. As did Pancho Villa's, the Terrazas' power grew with Chihuahua's increasingly predominant role in the nation's life. As most powerful northern family, they were in the best position to exploit the United States' strong end-of-the-century economic expansion.

The revolutionary movement in the region grew out of social mobilization against this powerful oligarchy. Members of the urban middle class, in fact, joined this movement, as did agricultural day workers, renters, and small landowners burdened by debt and blocked from competing in other regional markets. The revolution also swept up all those workers who performed odd jobs in forestry and local commerce, such as mule drivers, as well as unemployed textile and mine workers and those who drifted back and forth over the US border in search of a better life.

*A* photograph taken at the dawn of the new century: the old dictator at the apex of his power, seemingly solidly in control.

### Madero Leads the Rebellion against Díaz

During the regime of Porfirio Díaz, there were no true opposition parties. Dissent was expressed by means of newspapers and announcements that were printed under difficult conditions. But while rural revolts provoked by the seizure of communal lands were common in the late nineteenth century, the first significant protests by factory workers were not seen until 1906. A labor-based anarchist group formed around Mexican Liberal Party leader Ricardo Flores Magón tried to impart a "social revolutionary" character to these factory protests. Its leaders, in fact, created the first union-based groups in the mines of Cananea in Sonora and in the textile factories of the Orizaba region, in Veracruz; their organized strikes were harshly repressed.

Given the weakness of the labor movement, many workers, still tied to agricultural activity, abandoned the mines and factories, in search of other occupations. Several leaders of this party, such as Antonio Villarreal, a teacher, and Antonio Díaz Soto y Gama, a lawyer and one of Zapata's most active political collaborators, joined the various revolutionary groups. Many agitators and sympathizers also participated in the insurrections of 1910–1911 in the north.

With the presidential elections of 1910, Díaz's opposition gathered around Francesco Madero, who revived the platform of liberal constitutionalism, and supported the return to the principle of term limits for all posts political and administrative. Over the course of 1909, he began a political campaign against Díaz in both of the northern states and the central plateau; insisting on the connection between constitutional government and economic progress, he assembled a broad consensus.

In April of 1910, a congress of opposition organizations convened in Mexico City. The congress nominated Madero for the presidency, and proposed the adoption of economic and social measures that ranged from supporting credit for agricultural activity to labor legislation. The new movement demanded respect for local political autonomy and free suffrage – a request summarized in the slogan "true suffrage, not re-election" – as well as administrative reform.

The government of Porfirio Díaz responded with a heavy and repressive hand to the active electoral campaign of Madero. On the evening of June 16, 1910, shortly before the election, Madero was arrested in Monterrey and accused of mobilizing public opinion against the president; he was sent to the border city of San Luis Potosí. At the same time, many supporters of Madero were placed under arrest or forced into exile, and the opposition press was silenced.

*The principal demand of Díaz's opponents was that of free suffrage; they denounced on numerous occasions the intrigues and hierarchical control that allowed officials of the Díaz regime to maintain their positions of power.*

## THE PLAN OF SAN LUIS POTOSÍ

The political motives that prompted Madero to organize the revolt against Díaz were brought to light in the Plan of San Luis Potosí. In this document, Díaz's leading opponent drew attention to the old regime's reliance on force rather than law:

"The legislative power, as well as the judiciary are entirely subordinated to the executive; the division of powers, the sovereignty of the states, the liberty of the communes, the rights of citizens are affirmed only in our Constitution; in reality, however, in Mexico, it is martial law that prevails; justice, instead of protecting the weak, serves only to legitimize the improprieties forced upon the weak by the powerful; judges, instead of acting as representatives of justice,

are agents of the executive branch, whose interests they serve faithfully; the houses of congress express only the wishes of the dictator; it is he who nominates the state governors, and they, in turn, outline and impose municipal authority with similar methods. The entire mechanism — administrative, judiciary, and legislative — responds to a single will — that of General Porfirio Díaz, who, during his long administration, has shown his fundamental guiding principle to be that of retaining power at all costs." ■

The outcome of the June 26th elections seemed to sanction Díaz's victory, but his opponents gathered substantial documentation indicating the government's political manipulation in many states and they requested that Congress annul the election. Madero successfully escaped from Mexico and headed to San Antonio, Texas, joining other exiles who had decided to support the awaited democratization of political life and the re-establishment of a greater rule of law. A plea is launched – known as the San Luis Postosí Plan – encouraging armed rebellion against Díaz. The revolt broke out in Puebla on November 20, 1910, and continued to spread.

*Francisco Madero (on the left), head of the movement opposing the re-election of Díaz for the seventh time, united a vast array of forces; his movement contributed to the dictator's fall from power.*

After several failed attempts to organize in the urban areas of central Mexico, the core of the rebel group became concentrated in Chihuahua, where the effects of stagnation in the mining sector, caused by the international financial crisis of 1907, were more severely felt, and where the number of combatants immediately became very high (about 5,000). The main local political organizer was Abraham González, the cultivated leader of a rural middle class that had been weakened by the domination of the Terrazas. The popular leader with a greater following was Pascual Orozco, from a family of small Guerrero farmers.

Through the first months of 1911, the rebellion remained localized, dispersed, and without true coordination. Lacking arms and munitions, the natural instinct of the northerners, who knew the land and the horse, was to oppose the forces of the federal army with their mobility. In just a few months, the rural revolts spread gradually along the western cordillera from Chihuahua to Sinaloa and Tepic, near Zacatecas, and along the eastern cordillera of the state of San Luis Potosí to Tlaxcala and Morelos, in central Mexico. The insurrection fomented by Madero immedi-

*In the state of Morelos, Emiliano Zapata acquired prestige and power by insisting upon the need for agrarian reform that would return land to indigenous villages.*

ately makes clear the extent and strength of popular aspirations to possess land, especially where large landholders had expropriated communal lands from native villages, or blocked attempts by small landholders to enlarge their properties.

### The Madero Presidency

With rebellion spreading and the political crisis worsening, the Díaz regime reached an agreement with Madero on May 21, 1911 at Ciudad Juárez that stipulated the resignation of Díaz and his vice president and appointed the lawyer and diplomat Francisco Leon de la Barra provisory president, with the charges of scheduling new elections, offering amnesty to those accused of the crime of sedition, and overseeing the dissolution of the revolutionary forces.

Of the approximately 60,000 armed insurgents, half returned to their previous occupations, and many were dismissed with compensation; the combatants were offered the possibility of joining the rural police force, the *rurales,* a corps of volunteers commanded by former officers and instituted in 1857 as a national guard to maintain order in the countryside. In the

## ZAPATA'S AYALA PLAN

The Ayala Plan, presented by Zapata on November 25, 1911, is the most significant text of the revolution, from a social viewpoint. It established the need to return to the farmers the communal lands expropriated from them by the large landowners. Article 7, in particular, states: "Given that, in the great majority of villages, Mexican citizens do not even own the land they walk on, they are incapable of improving, even to a minimal extent, their social condition; nor are they able to devote themselves to industry or agriculture, because the land, the mountains, and the water are concentrated in just a few hands; it is, therefore, decided that a third of this monopoly be expropriated by means of indemnity agreements to wealthy landowners, and that it be distributed to villages or citizens who are unable to demonstrate ownership through ancient rights. This "third part" will constitute the *ejidos* (collective nuclei) – colonies, legal funds for the villages, for the planting of crops, or whatever else might lessen the poverty and increase the well-being of the Mexican people." ∎

northern states, over 1,000 rebels were accommodated in this way, in various military units.

Complying with the accords agreed to in Ciudad Juárez, Porfirio Díaz presented his resignation, and on May 27, 1911, embarked for Europe from the port of Veracruz. The provisional government of Francisco Leon de la Barra, formed with Madero's cooperation, only lasted a few months, until new elections were held in October. On June 7, Madero was greeted with jubilation in the capital, and, after winning the election on November 6, was installed as constitutional president. The restoration of state authority and the resumption of political life led, however, to new conflicts. The rebellion continued in the countryside, as did workers' demands. And in the course of local elections, conflicts arose between supporters of Madero and those still faithful to Porfirio Díaz.

The rural revolts that took place between 1911 and 1912 constituted one of the determining events of the political crisis of Madero's new government; for, in order to control them, he reinforced the army, which in a short time outstripped the power of the civil authorities. In 1912, expenditures on the military doubled and the number of conscripts tripled the 20,000-man total of 1910.

In reality, during this phase, no locally-based movement succeeded in becoming a force at the national level; the only possible exception was the peasant army led by Emiliano Zapata, in Morelos, which clearly influenced political events, both because of its cohesion and its nearness to the capital.

Zapata, born in 1873 at Anenecuilco, a village of barely 400 in the small state of Morelos, came from a family of farmers; in 1909, he was elected president of the local council. In sympathy with the Madero rebellion, Zapata had led, autonomously, a revolt aimed at regaining control of communal lands that had been taken, over time, from indigenous villages.

When, in 1911, the question of demobilization was posed, Zapata obtained an agreement that guaranteed him the title of head of rural police of the region, and agreed, in an accord with Madero, to take on the charge of confronting the agrarian question. But the

*This cartoon of a priest is one of thousands of engravings left to us by José Guadalupe Posada, a Mexican artist who portrayed the major events of the revolutionary epoch.*

agreement was not kept, and in the course of 1911, repression against the farmers' movement in Morelos grew ferocious. The break between Zapata and Morelos, at this point, became irreconcilable, and on November 25, the former issued a proclamation, the Ayala Plan, which called for a national revolution to secure the farmers' demands.

The Madero government came to an end in February 1913, after a convulsive ten-day period, between February 9 and 18, known as the *decena trágica*.

The old supporters of the previous regime and the conservatives, fearing a further political radicalization, mistrusted Madero and supported any conspiracy that might lead to his downfall. At dawn on February 9, an attempted coup d'état broke out, led by a group of soldiers. The British and Spanish ambassadors, sympa-

*Revolutionary troops occupy Ciudad Juárez during the early months of 1911. The north was the primary base of rebel forces which, united with Madero, began an attack against the regime's army.*

thetic toward Madero and his policies, tried to pressure the American representative Henry Lane Wilson. Wilson, in violation of the directives of his own government, which forbade interference in the internal affairs of Mexico, instead favored an agreement with the conspirators, and openly supported General Victoriano Huerta, a key figure in the federal army, who had been the pillar of social and political order under Porfirio Díaz.

On February 18, Madero was arrested in the presidential palace and a complex series of negotiations began that were intended to lend legitimacy to the coup and to force Madero's resignation. Madero was driven into submission and, by some constitutional legerdemain, Huerta was named president of the republic within a matter of hours. Despite a promise of safekeeping, Madero and his vice president were assassinated on the night of February 22. Huerta circulated the official version that the two men were killed in the course of an attempted escape.

The assassination of Madero, and the illegality and trickery with which Huerta acted, sparked the immediate formation of a resistance movement that opened the next phase of the revolution, in which popular movements, in particular that led by Villa, assumed a determining role.

*Charged with quelling the revolts that broke out in various locations between 1911 and 1912, General Victoriano Huerta was at the heart of the coup that overthrew Madero.*

## HUERTA: THE REACTION AGAINST MADERO

**B**orn in 1854 in Cototlan (Jalisco) to an indigenous farming family, Huerta completed his studies at Mexico City's military college, and later collaborated in the army commission charged with preparing cartographic samples of the nation. After 30 years of active military service, he settled in Monterrey, working as a civil engineer. Inactive during the electoral campaign against Díaz, he was re-called to military service in April 1911, and escorted the convoy that brought the deposed dictator to Veracruz, to depart for his exile. Huerta then commanded the army sent to Morelos to repress the Zapata movement. In 1912, he led the troops sent to put down the revolts in Orozco and Chihuahua. After the attempted coup of February 9, 1913, Madero named him military commander of the

capital, with the task of opposing the conspirators — but Huerta turned out to be in league with them. Following the arrest and assassination of President Madero, he became head of the counter-revolutionary government. Defeated on July 20, 1914, he fled the country. After several months in Spain, in April

1915, he reached the United States, proposing to re-establish, with the old supporters of Porfirio Díaz, a conservative government in Mexico. Arrested by American authorities in New Mexico at the end of June, he was imprisoned in El Paso, Texas, where he died in the middle of the following January. ∎

# Chapter 2

# FROM BANDIT
# TO REVOLUTIONARY

UNITED AT THE OUTBREAK OF THE REVOLUTION WITH
MADERO'S FORCES IN THEIR STRUGGLE AGAINST HUERTA,
PANCHO VILLA WAS THE POPULAR LEADER WITH THE LARGEST
FOLLOWING IN THE NORTH. IN A SHORT TIME, HE SUCCEEDED IN
MAKING CHIHUAHUA HIS POWER BASE AND BUILDING A
FORMIDABLE AND EFFICIENT MILITARY MACHINE.

Vamonos con Pancho Villa! – "Let's go with Pancho Villa!" – was the cry the popular classes in northern Mexico took up in 1913, to show their commitment to the revolution and the struggle against the Huerta government. Rafael Muñoz, a writer who witnessed Mexico in transformation, used the slogan as the title of a novel that enjoyed wide popularity during the 1930s. Echos of Villa's adventures run through the stories of Mexico's contemporary writers, more than those of any other revolutionary leader. Mariano Azuela, who began a literary cycle on the Mexican revolution and is author of the novel, *Los de abajo* (The Outcast), published in 1915, portrays Pancho Villa as a gentleman bandit.

*In 1912, Pancho Villa was arrested by Victoriano Huerta and brought by train to Mexico City, where he was imprisoned. But after a few months, he escaped and returned to the north, to organize his army.*

The image of Pancho Villa oscillates, in fact, between two poles: that of a criminal bandit and that of an angel fulfilling the hopes of the oppressed. These two images present a paradox that cannot be resolved, and such was the role he played in the revolution. He was an outlaw who became the expression of a people. He controlled vast territories, armed the unemployed, assembled a professional army of 50,000 men, and was courted by the president of the United States as a possible governmental leader.

Marte R. Gomez, a Mexican politician and first-rate scholar between the wars, compared Villa to a character in a Balzac novel: "With difficulty could one have found a protagonist who was at once generous and implacable, as full of love as he was full of hate, as ready to obey as to be proud enough to impose his will at any moment in his tormented life, astute enough to intuit the concrete dangers that threatened him, yet sufficiently naïve to be ensnared by the intrigues of those who would lead him to believe himself superior to others; and at the same time, able to determine the destiny of the country."

It was only after 1913 that Villa became central to the nation's life, when he contributed decisively to the defeat of the federal army, the principal instrument of the old regime and the conservative front. In the next

*P*ancho Villa surrounded by his elite guard, which was composed of roughly hewn men from Mexico's northern regions.

two years, Villa created a vast political movement and achieved great popularity, even among the US public. In early 1914, a cinematographic society filmed him directing his army; by May 1914, *The Life of General Villa* was complete. His military feats became legendary through popular ballads called *corridos*, and remain to this day imprinted in the collective memory, evidence of the widespread desire for social redemption.

Soon, however, Villa's own story followed the defeat of the popular revolution. The military debacle of the summer of 1915 signaled a return to his origins as a violent and indomitable warrior. The revolutionary civil war of 1914–1915, which placed Villa in opposition to Venustiano Carranza, the Maderist governor of Coahuila who rebelled against Huerta, remains one of

*The army organized by Pancho Villa between 1913 and 1914 constituted a powerful force that, within a short time, defeated dictator Victoriano Huerta's federal troops in a series of memorable battles.*

the most controversial episodes in Mexican history. At its core lies a fundamental disagreement about the type of political structure best suited for the country.

Various international problems compounded the civil war; primary among these were relations with the United States and which side to take in the European conflict that was itself developing into war. By the fall of 1915, Villa lost political and military control of the country. To explain this, one cannot ignore differences of the personalities involved – Carranza was cultured and possessed both political experience and a profound sense of the state; Villa lacked formal education and operated on impulse. But neither can one reduce to personalities the complexity of a power struggle between groups divided both by ideology and by region.

### The Leader of the Revolution in the North

When Villa leapt into the center of national life, little was known about him. Some information was eventually pieced together by his collaborators and journalists who knew him, such as writer and biographer Martín Luis Guzmán, and the American socialist John Reed, who left us, in his historical novel *Mexico in Revolt*, a lively portrait of the rebel's world. Guzman's apocryphal *Memories* remain somewhere between history and legend; single episodes, even banal ones, have become part of the myth.

*M*exico's natural landscape, a backdrop to Villa's activity, also appears in Mexico's muralist tradition, as seen in the Offering, *by Diego Rivera, a fresco at the Ministry of Public Education in Mexico City.*

Villa was born in 1878 to a family of renters in San Juan del Rio in the state of Durango. His early adult life already suggested the man ready to act against injustice. At the age of seventeen, he shot and wounded the owner of the hacienda where he worked with his family: this man had raped his younger sister. Wanted by the forces of justice, Villa was then obliged to go into hiding. It was during this time, while he lived in the borderlands of Chihuahua, that he acquired the experience that would make him a guerrilla and a popular leader. At first, he was a cowhand near San Andres, then worked as a miner at Parral, eventually moving to the city of Chihuahua: these both became important locations for his subsequent initiatives. In the process of searching for work and avoiding arrest, he changed his name, from Doroteo Arango to Pancho (the diminutive of Francisco) Villa. His choice was based on the fact that his father was the illegitimate son of Jesus Villa, a well-to-do gentleman of Basque origin. And thus, Pancho Villa became a bandit sought by the authorities. With the revolution, the term "bandit" no longer meant a simple criminal: it could mean a popular rebel. The word "bandit," spoken indulgently by some and distastefully by others, meant generally a political figure of humble origins, but also someone with an aura of violence about them. Villa, in becoming the leader of a broadly based social movement, transgressed simply

*Villa's popularity spread beyond the borders of his country. In 1914, the "Mexican Robin Hood," a name given him by the movie houses, signed a contract for $25,000 with the Mutual Film Corporation (advertisement at left) giving exclusive rights to film his exploits; the contract forced Villa not only to stage daylight attacks, but also, to simulate battles against enemy troops.*

by stepping out of the framework of a society rigidly divided by class. But the term "bandit," as applied to Villa after 1915, also suggested the weight of his shortcomings, underscoring his inability to become a truly modern political leader or to realign his movement to make it a more effective revolutionary force.

Pancho Villa, like many other local popular leaders, began his activity during the revolt of November 20, 1919, which Madero had fomented against Díaz. While active in Chihuahua, Villa remained, however, in the background. Working with Abraham González and the Maderist faction of the city, he created an armed nucleus. After launching an assault against the village of San Andres, west of the capital, he initiated a series of battles aimed to cut off the flow of supplies to federal troops, and to obtain additional weapons. Villa retreated to the south, toward Satevo, to organize other groups that would later unite with those who fought in the northern districts of the state. There, in February 1911, Madero arrived to establish a bridgehead and supervise Díaz's retreat from a position of force. Two months later, Villa was a hero in the capture of Ciudad Juárez by Madero's supporters.

With the demobilization following the fall of the dic-

## THE BALLAD OF THE REVOLUTION

The *corrido* is an epic narrative genre in quatrains, with variable rhyming. A popular ballad accompanied by an insistently repeated musical motif, the *corrido* narrates various events, from the passionate to the historic, from crimes to misfortunes (*mañanitas*). Of ancient origin, the *corrido* became a popular expression of the revolution of 1910 – for every important incident, person, event, or battle, a ballad was born. These anonymously written songs were a genuine manifestation of the creativity of popular participation. This *corrido* celebrates the taking of Zacatecas, a battle in which Villa's forces helped defeat the federalists. Here, a few verses:

"Now I sing to you these verses,
whose words are in ink,
now I sing to you all
how we took Zacatecas.
In nineteen hundred and
     fourteen,
on June the twenty-third,
Zacatecas was conquered,
between the hours of five and
     six.
Cried Francisco Villa,
at Calera station,
"Let's go help out
Don Pánfilo Natera."
It had already been a few days
since they had been fighting,
when the general arrives,
and places himself in command.
When Pancho Villa arrives,
he prepares them for action,
and to each combatant,
he gives an order.
This is how Francisco Villa spoke,
In command of the battalion,
And the fighting starts,
when the cannon fires." ∎

tator, Villa returned to the city of Chihuahua, where he opened a butcher shop, became a livestock trader, and legalized his union with Luz Corral.

After the dictator's departure, Abraham González was elected governor of Chihuahua. He adopted several reform measures on administrative practices, fiscal matters, and public education, but life in the region was far from tranquil.

In March 1912, Pascual Orozco, moved to action by local rebels, rose up against Madero. Many in Chihuahua were disappointed in the rate of social change and wary of Madero and his upper-middle-class supporters. The federal army was mobilized against the Chihuahua revolutionaries. Villa first joined the volunteer corps organized by Madero's brothers in the cotton-growing region of La Laguna, in support of the federal army stationed at Torreón under the command of Huerta. Next he aligned himself with Madero's supporters in Parral, who also supported Governor Abraham González.

After Orozco's defeat, Villa was accused of insubordination and wanting to act outside of the normal military channels, and Huerta ordered his execution. The furious intervention of the Madero brothers spared him the death penalty, but he was nevertheless sent, under escort, to the capital, and placed in military prison to

*Mobility helped insure the early success of the revolutionaries. Moving by train, with their horses, from one region to the next, they were able to seize vast expanses of territory from Huerta's federal troops.*

*Bandit and head of a popular revolt. This double interpretation of Villa's exploits has contributed to his mythic identity.*

await trial. But weren't Huerta and Villa allegedly on the same side – the side of Madero's supporters? Some say that Villa stole a purebred mare, whose breeder enlisted Huerta's help in getting it back. In any case, Villa remained in prison in Mexico City for several months. Impatient with the legal process, which seemed to have stalled, he escaped at the end of December with the assistance of a court employee. After a journey by train and boat through the eastern regions of the country, he reached El Paso, Texas in early 1913, just as the coup staged by Huerta placed the nation in a grave political crisis.

### The Rebellion against Huerta Spreads

In February 1913, just a few weeks after Huerta's installation as president of the republic, rebellion broke out. Protests led to repression, arrests of Maderist politicians, and the shutdown of several newspapers. The strongest opposition, however, came from the governors of the several states: They refused to recognize the new government. Huerta forcefully deposed the governors of San Luis Potosí, Aguascalientes, and Sinaloa. Before being deposed himself, the Maderist governor of Sonora, José María Maytorena, escaped to Tucson, Arizona, citing health reasons; but that state remained solidly in the hands of his supporters.

In the state of Chihuahua, the situation became critical. Abraham González was arrested on February 22, 1913, and forced to step down. In his stead, the region's military commander was installed, an action which, again, mobilized the people. Shortly afterward, while allegedly being moved to the capital, Gonzalez was betrayed and killed. The local Maderistas, thus lost their primary leader, while Huerta, to defuse the situation, attempted to appease Pascual Orozco's troops by promising to place the state government in their hands. But this was an unnatural alliance that could not last. On March 9, Villa clandestinely crossed the Río Grande to return to Mexico, and several days later, reached San Andres, reorganized his men, and within a few months became the principal revolutionary leader of Chihuahua.

The governor of Coahuila, Venustiano Carranza, declared himself in the meantime to be in open rebellion against Huerta. On March 26, 1913, he launched a seven-point program, the Guadalupe Plan, calling the nation to armed revolt against the usurpation of power by Huerta, and in favor of the restoration of legitimate constitutionality. He thus became the political head of the revolution, which, as a result of his appeal to constitutionality, became known as the "Constitutionalist Revolution."

The revolutionary groups of the north initially recognized the authority of Carranza, who moved to Sonora in order to gather forces to defeat Huerta. For the rest of the year, the various insurgent leaders attempted to consolidate their power in their respective regions. The arrangement for the next phases of the revolution thus unfolded, with Coahuila the base of Carranza's political force, Sonora that of his collaborators, and Chihuahua the political domain of Pancho Villa.

## CARRANZA AND THE GUADALUPE PLAN

Venustiano Carranza was born in 1859 at Cuatro Cienegas, a small rural town in Coahuila. Eleventh of fifteen children in a family of liberals who opposed the powerful supporters of Porfirio Díaz at the turn of the century, Carranza began his career as a mayor; he was subsequently designated deputy of the state assembly, and then senator of the republic. A supporter of Madero, in 1911, he became governor of Coahuila. In a region unmarred by serious social conflicts, Carranza created a network of loyal collaborators, became leader of the constitutionalist group, which adhered to the principles of the founding document of 1857, and maintained unquestioned political legitimacy.

His Guadalupe Plan asked for non-recognition of Huerta, incited rebellion, and stated: "**4.** Citizen Venustiano Carranza, constitutional governor of the state of Coahuila, shall be named commander-in-chief of the army that will lead our cause to victory; he will organize it, forming an army that will be "constitutionalist."

**5.** As soon as the constitutionalist army occupies Mexico City, Venustiano Carranza, or his successor in command, will be named provisory head of the executive branch.

**6.** As soon as peace has been established, the provisory president of the republic will immediately convoke general elections, thereafter consigning power to the citizen to be elected." ∎

**V**ictoriano Huerta, Emilio Madero (brother of the president), and Pancho Villa (seen from behind) in a photo taken in May 1912, after the three had quelled the revolt of Pascual Orozco in the state of Chihuahua. But their collaboration would be short-lived.

Having re-established contact with the old revolutionary core of Parral, Villa launched a series of ambushes to obtain arms and supplies from Huerta's troops. At the end of May, Carranza named him general of the new constitutionalist army, even though the two had never met (and would not until the end of the following year).

That summer, the fighting troops of Chihuahua succeeded in gaining control of a large part of the state, but federal troops maintained firm control over Ciudad Juárez and the state capital. The federal army had a real defensive capability, but was inept at mounting an offensive operation. In his struggle against the rebels, Huerta had to confront two serious problems. First, conscripts were deserting en masse, and Huerta was unable even to relieve the troops because of the general political climate; second, he was strapped financially, and the US failure to recognize his government forced him to turn to Europe. He was forced to impose a series of forced loans on business owners, and

## THE NORTHERN DIVISION

**I**n Martín Luis Guzmán's *Memorias de Pancho Villa,* written in 1938, Villa describes the birth of his army: "In the La Loma junta, I said to all of the bosses, 'Gentlemen, in a time of war, nothing is accomplished if one is not capable of commanding and obeying. When our forces come together to form a large number, the leaders of all the group must choose, among themselves, one who has the responsibility of commanding.... We must, therefore, in my opinion, name a boss who will guide us, one who, with his authority, will impart to our forces the organization necessary to advance the campaigns. I believe, in the absence of opposing opinions, that we must name, with the rank of general, my compatriot Tomás Urbina, or General Calixto Contreras, or myself.' Others spoke after having heard me. But since no one either spoke in clear terms, or expressed any dissent, Juan Medina stood up and explained why he believed it proper to organize our troops into a single division, and to choose me as general. All accepted his proposal, and from that moment, I, Pancho Villa, was named head of the *División del Norte*, which was constituted at that moment. This took place on September 29, 1913, the date on which I took the first steps toward organizing the *División del Norte*." ∎

required banks to relinquish their gold reserves – moves that, not surprisingly, alienated some of his sympathizers.

In the fall of 1913, the federal armies regained control the northern cities, but it was Villa – to whom, in September, the various brigades entrusted their operational command – who delivered the decisive blows. Around Torreón, he assembled the *División del Norte*, the revolutionary army with which Villa

came to be associated. In concert with groups active in Durango, he decided to advance on Torreón, the nerve center of the cotton-growing region of La Laguna and the strategic railroad center of the north, in an effort to isolate Chihuahua from central Mexico, and cut off all forms of re-supply.

Villa and his forces occupied Torreón on October 1, appropriating many war supplies, including ten cannons and, most importantly, about 40 locomotives, along with many other rail cars, which begin to give his army a great deal of mobility.

### Villa: Leader of Chihuahua

Control of the rail lines turned out to be essential in order to guarantee movement in sparsely populated areas, and to cover the great distances between urban centers. The city of Chihuahua, in fact, is about 280 miles from Torreón, which in turn is about 680 miles from Mexico City. Interrupting the main rail arteries rendered much more difficult the dispatching of reinforcements to the northern outposts of the federal army. Villa was also able to rely on the cooperation of the rail workers, who were some of his most precious allies. The conquest of Torreón greatly increased his reputation.

Villa, though, left control of the region to the local bosses, entrusting them with the job of holding out as

*At the beginning of October 1913, Pancho Villa's División del Norte proved its effectiveness, conquering the city of Torreón.*

*Alvaro Obregón, brilliant strategist of the constitutionalist army, led the rebellion against Huerta in the state of Sonora, in mid-1913.*

long as possible, while he tried to occupy the city of Chihuahua. In the meantime, he imposed obligatory loans on the banks of Torreón, and confiscated 7,000 tons of already-warehoused cotton, one-third of the annual mean production, which he later sold to the United States. He completed a series of diversionary actions around the city of Chihuahua, which continued to be controlled by federal troops. For example, in one quintessential Villa action, on November 15, he took control of a train north of the state capital, and changed its course toward Ciudad Juárez, arresting telegraph workers at the intermediate stops along the way, but not before having them announce that the train had arrived empty... a mix of audacity and cleverness that allowed him to catch each locale's garrison by surprise, and take possession of all the ordnance stored there.

After taking Ciudad Juárez by surprise, Villa completed a pincer maneuver against the city of Chihuahua, which was isolated from the south; but federal troops moved to the north in an attempt to block Villa and retake control of the frontier. The confrontation came to a head on November 25, 1913, in a battle at Tierra Blanca, a couple miles south of Ciudad Juárez. Villa, with the help of other commanders, repelled an attack, forcing the federal army to withdraw; from that point on, he remained in firm control of this border city.

The army's defeat demoralized the local governors loyal to Huerta, and the military commander decided to evacuate the state capital, which was isolated by rail from both the north and the south. On December 3, Huerta had federal troops evacuate to the east of Chihuahua, in the direction of Ojinaga, on the US border. The line of those evacuating included state functionaries, local notables, and all others who felt threatened. At the same time,

Villa ordered his men to withdraw from Torreón, preferring to mass his troops to confront Huerta's army.

From that moment, Villa became the ruler of Chihuahua, and on December 8, the junta of constitutionalist generals named him governor of the state. At the end of the month, he sent a number of brigades to Ojinaga to take control of the last bastion still in the hands of the federal troops, who, after a siege of several days, were forced to retreat across the border.

At the beginning of 1914, Villa, in complete control of Chihuahua, then returned to again occupy Torreón, which remained under his control for a year and a half. In the meantime, Alvaro Obregón, who would eventually assume important roles in both the military and politics of the constitutionalist alignment, dominated Sonora, Sinaloa, and Tepic in the west; Carranza's supporters held the northeast and San Luis Potosí.

The way to central Mexico was open and the federal army was on the point of collapse. During this period, Villa was the only revolutionary leader who could count on a powerful, well-financed army, and the only one capable of maintaining effective control of the territories under his administration.

*"Tierra y liberdad" appears clearly on this banner painted by Diego Rivera: it is the cry with which Emiliano Zapata and his movement oppose the Huerta regime and promote the distribution of land to the peasants.*

## PANCHO VILLA AS SEEN BY JOHN REED

**T**he following is John Reed's sketch of Pancho Villa, whom he observed in 1914, in Chihuahua: "[T]wo weeks before the advance on Torreón... the artillery corps of his army decided to present him with a gold medal for personal heroism... The officers of the artillery, in smart blue uniforms faced with black velvet and gold, were solidly banked across one end of the audience hall... From the door of that chamber, around the gallery, down the state staircase, across the grandiose inner court of the palace, and out through the imposing gates to the street, stood a double line of soldiers... The people of the capital were massed in solid thousands on the Plaza de Armas before the palace. '*Ya viene!*' 'Here he comes!' 'Viva Villa!'... 'Villa, the Friend of the Poor!' "The roar began at the back of the crowd and swept like fire in heavy growing crescendo until it seemed to toss thousands of hats above their heads. The band struck up the Mexican national air, and Villa came walking down the street.

"He was dressed in an old plain khaki uniform, with several buttons lacking. He hadn't recently shaved, wore no hat, and his hair had not been brushed. He walked a little pigeon-toed, humped over, with his hands in his trousers pockets. As he entered... he seemed slightly embarrassed, and grinned and nodded to a *compadre* here and there....

"It was Napoleonic!"

From: John Reed, *Insurgent Mexico* (New York: Simon & Schuster, 1969) 113–114. ∎

# Chapter 3

# THE REVOLUTION
# IN THE NORTH

BETWEEN 1913 AND 1915, THE STATE OF CHIHUAHUA WAS ENTIRELY UNDER THE CONTROL OF VILLA. BUT AFTER HUERTA'S DEFEAT, WHILE THE US GOVERNMENT HESITATED TO ARTICULATE ITS POLICY TOWARD MEXICO, THE FIRST DISAGREEMENTS EMERGED BETWEEN VILLA AND CARRANZA, WHO WAS THE KEY FIGURE IN THE CONSTITUTIONALIST ALIGNMENT.

After assuming military control of the state of Chihuahua, Villa attempted to consolidate his social and political control. He therefore decreed the confiscation of land and property from the local landowners. He promoted the formation of a centralized body to be administered by Silvestre Terrazas, a distant relative of the rulers of the state, an opponent of the Díaz regime, a director of a Maderist newspaper, and close collaborator of Villa's, as well as his delegate to the Chihuahuan government. This act, in a single blow, expropriated the holdings of the Terrazas and other families comprising the regional elite, and reinforced the consensus around the revolutionary Villa.

*The civil war that upset the country spread like an oil spot: from the northern states to those in the center and the south, soldiers, armed peasants, women, and even children were involved in the various fronts of the revolution.*

Most of the confiscated properties were entrusted directly to the revolutionary generals, or administered in their names. These immense properties, such as the San Luis hacienda, with nearly a million acres, or that of San Miguel de Bavícora, with over 860,000 acres, were destined for livestock production that would furnish the needs of the military. It was decided, after the military victory against Huerta, that the lands would be distributed to veterans of the revolution and to inhabitants of the old military colonies. The renters of small plots of land were promised pri-

*María Arías, known by the name of "María Pistolas," shows her sorrow at the assassination of President Madero in February 1913. Revolutionary legend has it that she was the only woman to enter the streets of Mexico City on that day.*

ority, if the land was sold; the poorest renters were granted permission to occupy these lands, as well as a one-year exemption from having to pay rent. The revenues obtained would cover the expenses needed to equip, arm, and maintain an army that had become quite professional. At the same time, Villa adopted other measures to provide for the distribution of meat and other needed goods at reasonable and controlled prices.

### A War Economy

While this happened in Chihuahua, an analogous situation developed in the rich, cotton-growing region of La Laguna. Villa reoccupied La Laguna in 1914, and immediately created a commission devoted to administering its economy. Expropriation, here, was limited to several Spaniards and declared supporters of Huerta. The haciendas generally remained under the governance of the administrators – partly because these holdings were much smaller than the livestock-breeding properties of Chihuahua, typically comprising a thousand acres of monoculture, which required specialized production techniques.

Thus, neither the management of the properties, nor the rental conditions of properties that had long

ago been consolidated, were changed, even though contracts favoring unemployed small-scale renters were to have been established. Cotton producers were required to sell all their cotton to a special commission, as well as transfer to this commission all earnings normally owed the owners of the property. The regional economy, in fact, continued to produce normally, and, the imposition of some surtaxes related to the war and inflation notwithstanding, the earnings of the small producers and renters declined by a

relatively small amount. The control of the La Laguna economy by Villa, however, placed the central Mexican textile industry in serious difficulties, even though cotton sold to the United States via Ciudad Juárez was in part reacquired and shipped by sea to Veracruz.

The revolutionaries were financed, without contracting international loans, through the unlimited printing of paper money, the imposition of export taxes, contributions from the war, and forced loans. So it was that the image of the revolution as a looting and pilfering operation came to form, for these practices formed the rule, rather than the exception. The first issuances of paper money without legal backing were registered under Carranza, in the spring of 1913; they subsequently multiplied by leaps and bounds in the various regions to an extent that a monetary crisis was provoked. This crisis was then used as a political weapon by various political groups in their respective territories.

At the end of 1913, Villa printed his own banknotes, immediately baptized *sabanas de Villa*, or Villa's "bed sheets." To these notes, others, designed with cari-

*In their own territories, the revolutionaries issued bank notes to meet administrative needs. Above are two samples printed in the states of Coahuila and Chihuahua, the latter under the control of Villa.*

catures from the popular imagination, were added; they flooded the nation at a steady pace until 1915. These bank notes were of low value; they amounted to a total of 10,000,000 pesos by May 1914. From this date, and throughout 1915, notes exceeding 400,000,000 pesos in value entered circulation. Halfway through the year, Villa began to furnish paper money to the revolutionary groups of central Mexico, and at this point, one million pesos per day were printed in Chihuahua.

At the same time, Villa, in addition to seizing the gold reserves of the Terrazas' bank, created the Bank of the State of Chihuahua with the purpose of controlling the printing of currency and of granting limited credit that would be guaranteed by expropriated properties. This bank became the fulcrum of all his financial operations. In short, he created a controlling administration, and the new currency was used in economic transactions and international commerce, even though, by so doing, he primed an inevitable slide toward inflation.

The political and social stability typical of the lands under Villa's control until 1915 was not replicated in other parts of the country during the revolutionary epoch. Also, there was a surprising absence of social agitation, given the fact that land expropriations were not accompanied by agricultural reform addressing the question of land distribution. Perhaps the area stayed relatively calm because Villa's firm control of Chihuahua made the danger of war seem distant; indeed, the great battles of the time occurred in Mexico's central region. And for that matter, the standard of living also generally improved.

But the absence of agrarian reform warrants further discussion, for pressures for land reform continued in many regions at this time. By the time Huerta fell in mid-1914, large landowners, with the exception of those in the south, had already fled the country, no longer expecting returns on their properties or profits on the sale of products, and fearing that their properties would never be returned to them. With the revolutionaries in control of the haciendas, this was the only moment in the entire arc of the revolutionary pro-

*The territories under Pancho Villa's jurisdiction were characterized by political and social stability unmatched in the rest of the country.*

cess that the possibility of changing Mexico's agrarian structure seemed present.

Villa decided to make the administration of the rural properties the financial base of his movement, both because of the revolutionaries' innate aversion toward the large landowners, and because of the difficulties in obtaining necessary means from foreign capitalists. As in many other regions, the revolutionaries, where they lacked direct control of the properties, requisitioned food and livestock, leaving the administrators with regular receipts that, in the end, were worthless. In this way, Villa put off agrarian reform, and he was imitated by other revolutionary bosses.

*In this painting by José Clemente Orozco, two* soldaderas *accompany the armies to the front in revolutionary Mexico.*

## LIFE DURING THE MILITARY CAMPAIGNS

The militant revolutionaries have written numerous novels, in which they describe the deeds and episodes of Mexico between 1911 and 1915. Here, a selection from *I Was a Soldier in a Cavalry Uniform*, by Francisco Urquizo, a collaborator of Venustiano Carranza's, who sketches a picturesque image of life during the military campaigns.

"Pay, I'll tell you – there was none! When the leaders issued the money they received from forced loans, they'd distribute it to each of us. But in fact, there was no need for money. For what? If we were in the mountains, or moving across the plains... to eat? We'd shoot cows and cook the meat; they'd give us flour to make flatbread, and everyone took care of himself. Sometimes the bosses would order us to prepare dried meat in quantity – with goat meat fried in fat. This meat lasted for months and even years without turning rancid. Forage for horses, yes. Without forage, there are no horses. In war, first the horses must eat, and then the men. The horse is your salvation; when it gets tired, it's finished, and it gets sores, then you have to abandon it, exchanging it for another that you take, wherever you are. The horse must be fresh and ready to carry a man... Clean clothes? Where do you get them? We stunk like lions. When our leaders would obtain loans by force, they would always provide an explanation: 'We'll pay after the victory.'" ■

From: Francisco L. Urquizo, *Fui soldado di levita, de esos de caballeria* (Mexico City: FCE-SEP, 1984) 160.

In Chihuahua, demands for land were less consistent and territorially more limited than the demands of those in the populous areas of central Mexico. The Chihuahuans were accustomed to performing a variety of jobs, since the agrarian economy was primarily cattle breeding – an activity requiring little manual labor beyond herding. Also, Villa guaranteed basic needs at a low price to city dwellers, unemployed miners and foresters, widows of revolutionaries, and orphanages; all these measures won him broad support. Villa's capacity to administer the regional economy even created aspirations of social ascent; at the same time, the formation of a strong revolutionary army brought its own related employment possibilities, as it needed a number of noncommissioned officers and people to help manage the logistics and needs of the large army.

In this way, a "new bourgeoisie" arose, composed of those administering the large livestock-breeding properties, managing the export of agricultural products, acquiring arms and munitions for the new popular army, and, especially, administering and maintaining relations with the United States. This last group had its origins in the Chihuahuan middle class and the Madero family and its collaborators – a family trusted by Villa. There was, then, little popular pressure for immediate agrarian reform. But this great asset of Villa's soon became a liability, for after suffering military defeat, these regions were no longer solidly under his dominion, and his grand army dissolved.

*Continually forced to relocate between battles, Pancho Villa's troops enjoyed an organized infrastructure that permitted them to build well-defended encampments in a brief time.*

### A Powerful War Machine

After the fighting at the end of 1913, Villa tried to organize his army and begin the march toward central

Mexico, along the line running from Ciudad Juárez to Mexico City, while the other movements, in Sonora and the northeast, continued to meet obstacles consolidating their territories. Chihuahua had already shown itself capable of furnishing conscripts; besides, Villa had at his disposal ordnance and artillery taken from Huerta's units, as well as new sources of finance.

His Northern Division had been transformed into a potent war machine. His main collaborator in both passion and intelligence was General Felipe Angeles, one of the few career military men who immediately took the side of the revolutionaries. Angeles' strategic sense improved the effectiveness of Villa's units. A true "greater state" was not formed, however, since the heads of the various brigades continued to nurture personal loyalties, and were always present at the head of their respective units in battle. For his part, Villa created a personal escort, the select cavalry corps known as the *dorados*, composed of young, strong men of the north who had become known for the courage they had demonstrated in the riskiest operations.

His ability to count on a solid administration in Chihuahua and to utilize rail convoys granted his army extraordinary mobility, which was crucial, given the great distances – often through arid expanses – they had to travel to reach the field of battle. In the local shops, cannons were quickly repaired, including the legendary "El Nino," which had been taken from the federals and hidden on a railroad car; even a hospital train, complete with beds, nurses, and doctors, was formed to care for the wounded. Such organization, furthermore, made it possible to transport work-

*Schooled in French military academies, Felipe Angeles was the brilliant strategist of the* División del Norte.

ers to various locations to repair the tracks, the bridges, the telegraph lines. Villa equipped a special wagon that became his lodging, as well as his operations center. Thus, he created, in a few months, a well-equipped army with abundant munitions and provisions; he gave his men dark khaki uniforms, Texas hats, and red bandanas to be worn around the neck. This was an army that would make a strong impression when, on December 6, 1914, it paraded victorious through the streets of Mexico City. On many occasions, federal conscripts taken prisoner and sent to Chihuahua were convinced to join Villa's army.

From the experiences of earlier revolts, as well as the organization of the federal army, Villa learned several lessons. For logistical reasons, when possible, he eliminated the presence of *soldaderas* – the women following the troops, whose job it is to prepare their meals – because they slowed the pace of the march. And in the cavalry brigades, each soldier was required to carry a minimum of provisions, to increase the mobility of the detachments.

*P*ancho Villa, front and center, indicated by a circle, among his dorados, his personal guards who protected him under any circumstances.

The chance to put this war machine to the test came in March 1914, when Villa decided to retake Torreón, Huerta's advance outpost. Villa left Chihuahua with fifteen trains, over 8,000 men, and about 30 cannons, with all auxiliary services. After reaching the region on March 22, he began a series of combined artillery and cavalry maneuvers that confirmed his tactical skill. After putting up a strenuous resistance, the federal army abandoned the city on April 3.

With the way to the center of the country now open, the circle tightened around the strongholds controlled by Huerta: Obregón, from the northwest, marched on Guadalajara; Carranza's men put their sights on San Luis Potosí; and from Torreón, Villa proceeded south, toward Zacatecas, about 250 miles away. All lines of action converged on Mexico City.

At this point, however, a strong disagreement arose between Villa and Carranza. The first of a number of disagreements among the revolutionary groups, this was the germ of the eventual break-up. Carranza wanted Villa to remain in the capital for a lengthy

*The rail convoys were a fundamental element in Villa's strategy: they assured him mobility and timeliness in his interventions in the various war theaters.*

period, in order to impose his political authority. In their first encounter in Chihuahua, in March 1914, Carranza tried to attenuate Villa's political and financial autonomy by replacing him with a new and weaker state governor. In truth, with Huerta's fall imminent, the political problem of how to construct the new government was beginning to assert itself much more concretely than ever before.

Pánfilo Natera, head of one of Villa's combat units, decided to attack Zacatecas on June 10. Carranza asked Villa to send only 5,000 men as reinforcements and proposed that he not lead the attack, but rather, that Natera, who was a native of the place, do so. It was Natera, he argued, who should enter the city and install himself as the new revolutionary political authority. Carranza's intent was to keep Villa from broadening his domain. Carranza's best card was his control over the coal mines of Coahuila, and Villa's need to provision himself with fuel for his trains.

*John Reed described a soldadera whom he met in his travels across Mexico: "She was a young [native] woman, about 25 years in age, with the stocky build of her race, but a thin waist because of the fatigue – a pleasing figure, with her hair in two long braids that reached her shoulders, and when she smiled, she displayed a row of teeth that were large and shiny."*

Villa, however, wanted for both tactical and military reasons to move with his entire division. Exerting his political weight and disregarding Carranza's wishes, on June 17 he moved against Huerta with 23,000 men.

Mountainous Zacatecas has none of the open expanses typical of the northern landscape. It is a well-defended fortress. There on June 23, the decisive battle took place. With perfect coordination of the artillery, infantry, and cavalry, Villa cut off all possible ways of escape for the federal troops. The entire operation, conceived by General Felipe Angeles, is viewed by history as a textbook maneuver. The federal troops were decimated, and the occupation of Zacatecas definitively opened the way to the capital for the northern revolutionaries. Mexico City was now less than 400 miles away, and the end of the Huerta government was in sight.

Villa, however, decided to return to Chihuahua rather than proceed south. This left the path open for Obregón's constitutionalists. Obregón, in fact, who ultimately negotiated the surrender of Mexico City, took credit for the operation. As Villa had slowly distanced himself from Chihuahua, political and military control of the lands he once held became more and more difficult. For this reason, he wanted to go home to reorganize the army, especially since the great artery joining the north and the capital was now freely passable.

*To counter Villa's forces during the battle of Zacatecas, Huerta did not hesitate to send child-soldiers into battle.*

### Relations with Woodrow Wilson's United States

From the outset of the revolution, the problem of international relations was quite complex. In the United States, the new Democratic administration of Woodrow Wilson, who was elected to office shortly after Huerta's coup d'etat of February 1913, immediately had to confront the thorny question of Mexican relations.

First Wilson excluded any possibility of annexing a part of Mexico, or setting up a protectorate, as had happened in the Caribbean after Cuba won its inde-

## THE BATTLE OF ZACATECAS

At Zacatecas, 23,000 men from various units of the *División del Norte* were involved, distributed all around the city, along with about 40 pieces of artillery. Reports of the encounter come from Felipe Angeles's diary. It is unanimously agreed that Zacatecas was the decisive action in bringing down Huerta. Federico Cervantes, like Angeles a former officer of the federal army who went over to the ranks of Villa, writes, "The battle presents all phases: preliminary patrolling, making contact with the enemy, circling the place, the orderly distribution of troops, the choice of emplacement and studied artillery disposition, extremely effective use of artillery in supporting the advance of the ground forces, the choice of a principal front of attack and the possibility of a reserve, regular progression, as foreseen, of the battle, systematic assault on the defenses, a final effort, and a follow-up so effective that the reserve forces annihilated the enemy troops in retreat." ∎

pendence from Spain in 1898, and in Central America during the century's first decade. Wilson remained convinced, however, of the need for a stable, democratic government, and tried to determine which of Mexico's leaders might best guarantee it.

Unlike the case for other Latin American nations, US interests in Mexico were not limited to a few strategic sectors in Mexico. Mining investments, the metallurgical industry (then in a stagnant period), export agriculture, livestock production, manufacturing, and commerce all played a role in determining US foreign policy. Disagreements between the European powers strongly influenced the positions taken by the respective governments in the Mexican crisis. For example, rivalries among British and US petroleum interests, in the end caused the English to favor the Huerta government, and the United States to oppose it. Also, the strong financial and commercial presence of Germany changed US conduct in Mexico after the outbreak of the First World War.

In Washington, the number of personal envoys, consular clerks with divergent opinions, and agents of various revolutionary groups clamoring for attention – not to mention the official diplomats! – made it such that relations between the two nations were entrusted to a plethora of informants and representatives, some more and some less official, who did little more than add to the complexity of the situation.

*Remington guns, produced in the US, were one of the most common weapons found among the various participants in the Mexican revolution. This advertisement praises their qualities and ease of use.*

Under these circumstances, Wilson arrived in the White House to face the question of recognition of the Huerta regime. Unlike England and other European nations, which did recognize Huerta at the end of March 1913, Wilson decided only to place an embargo on arms and weapons shipments to the contenders for power. The new administration also sought to

avoid becoming compromised politically by seeming, in a recognition of Huerta, to endorse the coup against Madero.

After a few months, it had to have been clear to Washington that the revolutionaries controlled the north. When, in the fall of 1913, Huerta dissolved the congress and held mock elections, Wilson's continued hesitation finally appeared inadequate. Despite many uncertainties, Wilson then decided to pay the utmost attention to the Mexican crisis. Soon after, he lifted the embargo on the constitutionalists, and endorsed a policy aimed at Huerta's removal from office.

Villa initially received the sympathy of the US government and press, both because he gave the impression of being capable of bringing the country under his control, and because his interests did not conflict with those of the US. In the north, many Mexican landowners, fearing expropriation of their goods, were anxious to sell their properties at low prices and place them under the titles of US citizens, in order to place them under diplomatic protection. At this point, the presence of American capitalists in the Mexican countryside became crucial, however difficult it may be to quantify this phenomenon. The alliance negotiated with the United States between 1913 and 1914 obliged the revolutionaries to respect the property of US citizens, but certain groups initiated various forms of confiscation that provoked protests and mistrust. Luis Terrazas, though, convinced that the situation would soon change, did not give up his immense holdings to American creditors, and this temporarily avoided diplomatic complications for Villa.

Several episodes aroused international furor, however. The complaints received by consular and diplomatic authorities regarding reimbursement for damage to foreign property and goods were the order of the day. In Chihuahua, protests by foreign citizens with money in the city's banks followed Villa's occupation of the provincial capital.

In February 1914, while Villa is at Ciudad Juárez, two events had great repercussions. Villa ordered the execution of English citizen William Benton, owner of

*P*resident Wilson's uncertainty with regard to the revolution stemmed mostly from his obligation to protect American interests in Mexico.

*In the south, Zapata's forces challenged Huerta; in the north, another challenge beside Villa's took shape: the "constitutionalist" movement, led by Venustiano Carranza, governor of Coahuila. But between Carranza and Villa, disagreements would soon arise.*

a hacienda and several mines between Durango and Chihuahua. Following an intense exchange of consular and diplomatic correspondence, Villa accused Benton of personal aggression; he ordered a summary trial of Benton post mortem, a second execution, and consignment of the cadaver. A short time later, a similar fate befell an American citizen accused of having collaborated with Huerta. Diplomatic representatives used these episodes to argue that the country was in uncertain hands, and that it lacked a government able to maintain law and order.

Over time, problems of this nature multiplied, and US consular representatives throughout Mexico often found themselves protecting citizens from other nations, spawning many controversies and accusations of interference. Among the episodes that gave Villa a bad name in international circles was the expulsion of many Spaniards from Chihuahua and Torreón, at the end of 1913 and then in 1914. Unlike other foreigners, the Spaniards were seen as a people "like" the Mexicans; in most cases, they had been rooted for many years in the country as administrators of rural properties, shop owners, and clerics. They were also well represented on civic committees in support of the Huerta government.

In this intricate situation, on April 21, 1914, 3,000 US Marines landed at the Mexican port of Veracruz. Using as a pretext a banal incident at Tampico between several federal troops and a group of US sailors, President Wilson tried to persuade Huerta, by both military and diplomatic means, to step down. The marines occupied the customs building, and the post and telegraph office, in order to stop the delivery of an arms shipment from Europe to federal troops. This action created a wave of patriotism that Huerta tried to exploit, recruiting men to fight the invaders.

While Villa saw the US action in a positive light, Carranza requested the withdrawal of foreign troops from Veracruz, separating the struggle against Huerta from the question of national sovereignty. Wilson used the occasion to try to arrange political mediation of the conflict by enlisting the support of several Latin American nations (Argentina, Brazil, and Chile). At the end of May, the representatives of these Latin American nations, the US, and Huerta, brought together by pressure from Britain, met at Niagara Falls. Carranza, as head of the revolutionary government, refused to send observers. Despite his natural inclination to look favorably on any measure designed to get rid of Huerta, he rejected the interference by outsiders in internal Mexican affairs.

The Niagara Falls meeting proceeded with the goal of reaching a compromise and appointing a provisory president acceptable to the United States and England. But with the advance of the revolutionary armies on the capital after the battle of Zacatecas, an accord was signed that provided for Huerta's resignation (tendered on July 8) and the naming of a new president, Francisco Carbajal, who, in turn, was forced to abandon the country on August 12.

Mexico City, gripped in the siege imposed by the constitutionalists and Zapata's forces, remained under the authority of its governor, Eduardo Iturbide. Obliged by Alvaro Obregón, commander of the revolutionary troops, Iturbide accepted terms of unconditional surrender of the garrison, which was manned by

*The patio of a provincial hotel at the beginning of the century, which mirrors the homes of the well-to-do during the colonial period.*

25,000 troops. So Obregón's constitutionalist troops gained free passage into the capital on August 15, 1914.

### The First Disputes between Villa and Carranza

The outcome of Wilson's international conference was immediately understood to be in doubt, as the problem of creating a government that might prove durable once again emerged.

In March, as the military victory loomed and the political question surrounding the formation of a new government became more pressing, relations began to falter between Villa and Carranza, who was beginning to gain a reputation as a national leader. The dispute between Villa and Carranza was not the only pressing matter, but it was certainly the most significant for the fate of the entire movement. Following the battle of Zacatecas and Villa's retreat to the north, several accords between the two leaders were reached, culminating in the so-called Torreón Pact of July 8, 1914. Villa made an effort to recognize Carranza as *Primer Jefe*, the first leader, of the constitutionalist forces, with regard to political and

LOS YANKEES EN VERACRUZ

*A cartoon depicting US sailors after their debarkation at Veracruz on April 21, 1914, by painter José Clemente Orozco.*

diplomatic questions.

In exchange, Carranza promised to recognize Villa's Northern Division as a force equal to the other revolutionary corps, and to entrust the command of the entire army to General Felipe Angeles. The generals of the Northern Division also asked (1) that they be admitted to the governing junta, (2) that an assembly of delegates (one for every 1,000 soldiers) for the new army be established, (3) that they play a role in developing the governing program, and (4) that none of the revolutionary leaders be a candidate in future presidential elections.

These accords made the final assault against the capital possible. But differences between the principal revolutionary groups remained, and by the end of the year, they found themselves embroiled in a cruel civil war that would cost 200,000 lives – many more than those lost in the preceding phases combined.

In the meantime, Mexican-US relations stalled. The US occupation of Veracruz continued through the month of November 1914, with Wilson still hesitating to choose sides between the revolution's protagonists. He maintained cordial relations with Villa, who, it seemed, might gain the upper hand.

**V**enustiano Carranza, between Sonoran governor José María Maytorena and Alvaro Obregón, commander of the fourth Sonoran battalion. The accord between Carranza and Maytorena proved short-lived.

## A PORTRAIT OF ALVARO OBREGON

**B**orn in 1880 to a family of small farmers in southern Sonora, Obregón became mayor of Huatabampo in 1911. During the revolution, Obregón played a role of primary importance. President of the republic between 1920 and 1924, he was re-elected in 1928; but on July 17 of the same year, just before assuming office, he was assassinated. Narciso Bassols – jurist, university lecturer, minister, and diplomat during the 1930s – provides an accurate portrait of Obregón: "In 1911 he was an arrogant young man, tall, bright-eyed, robust and happy. With an extraordinary memory, he retained a photographic image of events and of what was going on around him; with a fervid imagination, he took few things seriously, always seeking the clever, the ingenious.... His participation in the revolutionary process, his undeniable influence on people and events over the fifteen most turbulent years of Mexican life, gave him, little by little, without a theoretical background, without an abstract aim, without academic polish, a political personality that was, perhaps, the most representative of the epoch. Obregón's political ideas were practical, concrete, and capable of affecting the flow of a current that was transforming the country, and deciding the fate of violent contests, in which the participants played simultaneously with their own lives and the national destiny. ■

From: Narciso Bassols, *El Pensamiento politico de Alvaro Obregón* (Mexico City: El Caballito, 1976) 9–10.

# Chapter 4

# THE CIVIL WAR
# IN THE REVOLUTION

IN LESS THAN A YEAR, BETWEEN THE FALL OF HUERTA IN THE SUMMER OF 1914 AND THE GREAT BATTLE AT CELAYA IN APRIL 1915, VILLA'S STAR BEGAN TO DIM. PRESIDENT WILSON, WHO AT FIRST HAD SEEN VILLA AS A SORT OF "MEXICAN GEORGE WASHINGTON," SHIFTED HIS SUPPORT TOWARD CARRANZA.

W ith the fall of Huerta in the summer of 1914 came the collapse of the institutional base of the old social order. Fear began to materialize and "the tribulations of well-to-do families" grew, to use the words of the writer Mariano Azuela.

*One of the revolution's lasting images: The look of alarm on the face of a soldadera as she steps from a train.*

The party created by Madero in 1911, which had sought a renovation of political life, had disappeared. Legitimacy resided only in a number of revolutionary armies of mixed societal composition, and without solid ideological bases. Venustiano Carranza, whose allegiance lay first and foremost with the constitution, saw himself as the legitimate leader of the provisional government. The agreement the revolutionaries had made in the Torreón accords in July of 1914 provided for the convening of an assembly of all the divergent revolutionary forces. This assembly, though, was unable to create an authoritative and stable government. Through the fall of 1914, a power void developed, and the number of individuals claiming to represent the aspirations of all Mexicans multiplied.

In October of 1914, in Mexico City, Carranza upheld the agreement by convoking the "Convention of representatives, governors, and commanders of the revo-

*Zapata (below) created a revolutionary army (at right) that was nothing more than the armed league of the communes of Morelos, where agrarian reform was under way and the local authorities were elected by the people.*

lutionary constitutionalist army," to decide the future of the country. But if Zapata had never recognized Carranza's authority, it was now clear that neither Sonoran governor, José María Maytorena, nor Villa, found themselves in Carranza's camp, either. And Villa warned other revolutionary leaders to be wary.

In a short time, the revolutionaries, under Villa's military protection, would oust Carranza, name a new provisory president, and, for nearly a year, attempt to govern the country.

### Alliances on a Collision Course

The changing and complex plots that created fissures in the revolutionary movement were grounded in the political friction between Villa and Carranza, as well as in the differences between three places quite distant from one another: the Sonora border with the United States, Mexico City, and the port of Veracruz, which, after the American troop withdrawal (November 23, 1914), would become the seat of the Carranza government.

The Sonoran question went back to August 1913, when Maytorena, who had been elected governor during the Maderist epoch (when he was an advocate of local agrarian interests), again took charge. In his absence, the revolutionary heads had confiscated the properties of absentee owners; this had led to donations, mortgages, and sales favoring US citizens, in the hopes that the properties might be taken back in the form of an expropriation. With the return of Maytorena, measures were put in place to protect the properties of absentees, and block the sale of these properties to foreigners. In this way,

Maytorena hoped to avoid diplomatic complications and re-establish state control over its own territory.

At the same time, Maytorena opposed the fact that export taxes on livestock flowed to the provisory government of Carranza, who at that point had established himself in the capital of Sonora. Maytorena refused to deliver a portion of the state's revenues to Carranza, but the problem remained unresolved, because Carranza's supporters controlled the border crossings with the US (at Nogales, Naco, and Agua Prieta), and as a consequence, had the last word on international commerce.

Villa and Maytorena, for different reasons, feared that Carranza might gain control over the new revolutionary assembly, and change the local power structure. Alvaro Obregón, military commander of the constitutionalist army of Sonora, which was then occupying Mexico City, offered to mediate. Between the end of August and the end of September 1914, Obregón went twice to Chihuahua at the risk of being shot by Villa. Villa, on September 22, declared his refusal to recognize the authority of Carranza, and stated that representatives of the Northern Division

*Zapata's movement embodied the last hope of social redemption for the lower classes and peasants, who saw in agrarian reform and land distribution the preservation of their social and political dignity.*

would not participate in the assembly convoked in Mexico City; Maytorena did the same. For his part, Zapata asked that the social reforms, as formulated in his Ayala Plan of November 1911, be preliminarily accepted.

### A Power Struggle

The revolutionary front was divided. Villa's military force was approaching the capital. In Zacatecas, a third encounter with Obregón took place. Obregón moved to have the "Revolutionary Convention" trans-

ferred to the city of Aguascalientes, capital of a small mining state, just over 300 miles north of Mexico City. The Convention of Aguascalientes offered the revolutionaries a chance to exchange opinions for an entire month. Throughout, the city was a beehive of revolutionary leaders with their respective state leaders in

*A train carrying federal troops involved in a fire-fight with Zapata's forces in Morelos.*

tow. Carranza, however, did not participate; Zapata did not appear in person, and Villa controlled the outcome from outside. There was certainly no lack of discussion of the country's social and political problems, but no documents of consequence were immediately approved, and the legitimacy of the proceedings must have been in doubt, with so many of the main actors missing.

In the tumultuous fall of 1914, several attempts were made among the various parties to find a compromise solution that would lead to the installation of a legitimate authority who was recognized and independent of the revolutionary leaders. No organized political groups emerged, but attempts were made to resolve the situation by creating distance from both Carranza, the potential national leader, and Villa, who remained leader of the main armed branch of the revolution.

Gestures followed counter-gestures in rapid succession, and civil war seemed inevitable.

On October 1, approximately 80 representatives of governors and commanders of the revolutionary divisions met in the Chamber of Deputies in Mexico City. Excluded from this assemblage were representatives of Villa and Zapata, who decided to back Carranza as provisory head of the executive branch of the government, and continued to work through the assembly at Aguascalientes.

At the Convention of Aguascalientes, which opened on October 10 in the city theater, 152 delegates participated, of whom 37 were Villa supporters; 15 days later, Zapata's delegation of 26 arrived. On the evening of October 14, there was a ceremony in which loyalty to the constitutionalist army Convention was sworn; each delegate placed his signature on

*P*easant-farmers being assigned land, in a territory under Zapata's jurisdiction.

a tricolor flag decorated with the embroidered golden eagle. Pancho Villa, who chose not to be present at the opening of the congress, delegated his power to Roque González Garza, and appeared a few days later, asking that he be given the opportunity to swear his loyalty, as well; he made a brief speech to the applause of the delegates.

The assembly declared itself a sovereign organ, attributed constitutional powers to itself, adopted Zapata's agrarian program, and, after a lengthy debate, decided to deprive Carranza of his executive authority, and Villa of his command of the Northern Division. On November 1, Eulalio Gutiérrez, a revolutionary head of the mining zone to the north of Zacatecas, was elected the new president pro tempore of the republic. Thanks to Obregón's talents as a mediator, most of the votes of Carranza's supporters went to Gutiérrez, though those

of Villa's supporters went to another candidate.

The assembly debated in a climate of war, since the various generals in control of the surrounding countryside deployed units of their armies at strategic points; Villa, in particular, occupied Zacatecas, and was moving closer to Aguascalientes. The attempt to repair the falling-out between Villa and Carranza proved illusory. The latter rejected the Convention's deliberations, and pressured the various generals to pull back. Thus, on November 10, the assembly was declared to be in rebellion; subsequently, however, half of the representatives would slowly line up with Carranza.

On November 16, 1914, the meetings of the Aguascalientes assembly closed; a commission was charged with developing a reform program. A decision was made to march on the capital to install the new government, with Villa designated by Gutiérrez as commander-in-chief of the Convention army. Villa moved with 35,000 men toward the middle of the country, which was still under the control of Carranza supporters, and on November 30, he arrived at the outskirts of Mexico City, where Zapata's men had arrived in the meantime. Carranza then left the capital and ordered his men to evacuate, with as much of their ordnance as possible, in the direction of Ver-

*Diego Rivera, among the greatest of Mexican mural painters, painted a cycle of frescoes at the Ministry of Public Education in Mexico City, between 1923 and 1928. Above, a detail from* Sharpening the Machete.

## THE CONVENTION OF AGUASCALIENTES

On October 14, 1914, after his swearing-in ceremony, Antonio Villarreal, president of the assembly of Aguascalientes, delivered an emotional speech. He proclaimed that the revolution, "which is, more than anything else, social, and which was nourished and born of the wounded and famished earth, will not end, will not come to a conclusion, until slavery, which until a short time ago was present in Yucatan and the south, has been eradicated from our country, until hunger wages have disappeared, and until beggars who are capable of working, but must request alms because they cannot find work, are no longer present in our cities.

We must end *peonaje* (the practice of hiring day-laborers), and must work to increase salaries and reduce the number of hours in the work-day, and must work to have day and industrial laborers become citizens.... We should not be subject to the whims of the various *caudillos* (bosses) whose caprices lead us into war, but rather, to the coherence of principle, and laws of conscience. We must have the courage to say: before men come principles; we must have the courage to affirm that the deaths of bosses are preferred in order to safeguard the nation's liberty. Instead of shouting, "hooray" for those bosses who are still alive, who must still undergo the judgment of history, let's all raise our voices, "Long live the Revolution! This Sovereign Convention is solemnly opened." ∎

acruz. This portion of the gulf was in the hands of his supporters, though the city itself, the principal port of international trade, was still occupied by US troops.

For months, diplomatic notes crisscrossed between the United States and Mexico, resulting in the eventual withdrawal of the marines from Veracruz – a city that, in the meantime, saw 15,000 frightened refugees arrive to await transport to Europe. Negotiations, in the end, were conducted by Carranza's representatives; Villa did not appear in the region. On November 23, the 7,000 American soldiers finally left the city under the watch of Carranza, who immediately afterward declared Veracruz the capital of the republic and the seat of his provisory government. Carranza's installation at Veracruz, the abandonment of the Convention by Obregón, and the weakness of Gutiérrez's government were the primary obstacles that would thwart Villa's efforts to consolidate power on a national scale.

### Villa and Zapata in Mexico City

At Aguascalientes, no agreement was reached between Villa and Zapata's representatives, who had preferred to delay ratification of the Convention's decisions. At the end of November, the departure

*A group of delegates to the convention, held in the Morelos Theater of Aguascalientes between October and November 1914. Plagued by divisiveness among the revolutionary forces, the convention failed to become an effective governing organ.*

*The joint entry into Mexico City by the armies of Villa and Zapata on December 6, 1914, sealed a pact agreed to by the two revolutionary leaders. Below, the provisional governor, Eulalio Gutiérrez, is seated between the two revolutionaries at the banquet.*

from the capital by Carranza's supporters, and the numerous defections from the Convention's front re-opened the political problem of setting up a national government. On November 30, 1914, Villa reached the Tacuba station, at the doors of the capital, with 20,000 men and 18 trains. He immediately sent a delegation to talk with Zapata, whose troops had entered the city several days earlier, but later withdrew for fear of violence. The two popular leaders agreed to meet at Xochimilco, an area south of the capital that was controlled by Zapata's forces. Villa stayed in Mexico City only briefly; on December 10, he departed to consolidate the front at Guadalajara, returned twelve days later, and after just two more weeks in the capital, returned to the north. This was the most significant opportunity for an alliance between these two movements, but the bond holding them was weak.

## A PORTRAIT OF EULALIO GUTIÉRREZ

**V**ito Alessio Robles, secretary of the Convention, painted a colorful portrait of President Gutiérrez: "He was, without a doubt, one of the nicest and most colorful people at the Convention. Broad-shouldered, robust, large torso, short legs and enormous feet, his face was extraordinarily vivacious, with Tibetan or Mongolian traits, a smooth and descending moustache, and oblique eyes. He had been a goatherd until he was 12, and possessed all of the malice and diffidence of those who have lived in contact with nature. He later became a shopowner at Saltillo and at Concepción del Oro, where he dedicated himself to mining activities.... He and Carranza were the first to take up arms against Victori-

ano Huerta, and it was he who used enough dynamite to derail train convoys. With a gift of great intelligence, he was highly respected by the revolutionaries. His vivaciousness won much sympathy, as did his colorful jargon, peppered as it was with peculiar and off-color words. Majestically in his

element as he sat in the large chair of the Morelos Theater, he resembled a Mandarin. Everyone called him, affectionately, 'Ulalio.'" ∎

From: Vito A. Robles, *La Convención revolucionaria de Aguascalientes* (Mexico City: BINEHRM, 1979) 127.

Shortly after his initial arrival in Mexico City, Villa imposed a new government on provisionary President Gutiérrez, naming principal political and law enforcement officials. On December 3, with these new authorities present, he seized the presidential palace, announcing the new order to the citizenry by ringing the bells. Gutiérrez, without a political movement and a solid regional support base, found himself dependent on Villa, who made his decisions without consulting Zapata. Zapata, meanwhile, had his own agenda, as well as a 40,000-man army, and himself controlled vast areas around the capital.

The next day, a historic meeting occurred between the two popular leaders, who were accompanied by their various followers and escorts. The two leaders came from entirely different perspectives: Zapata represented a world of communal solidarity of the indigenous villagers; Villa, the solitary and individualist men of the north. This first meeting was surrounded by a festive climate that encouraged exchanges of opinion. The two spoke in private, and at length.

They set the groundwork for the collaboration of their respective armies, and Villa promised to furnish the military assistance badly needed by Zapata to continue his campaign in the south. On the political plane, Villa declared his support of Zapata's agrarian program, but both men put off addressing the problem of governance, though both were in favor of having a civilian elected to the presidency. They sealed the agreement with the decision to organize a triumphal entrance into the capital – their two armies united – on December 6.

The city joyously greeted the parade of these two revolutionary armies, which each numbered about 20,000 men. At its head were a cavalry squad from the southern army and a unit of *dorados*, followed by Villa and Zapata. Villa wore a dark blue uniform and a beret, while Zapata donned the typical gala dress of a Mexican horseman, with black pants, yellow jacket, and broad-rimmed hat. Infantry units of the two armies followed, with Zapata's soldiers in white cotton clothes, sandals, and pennants of the Madonna of

*The patron saint of Mexico, the Virgin of Guadalupe, was pictured on the banners of Zapata's forces.*

Guadalupe and Villa's, well-dressed and disciplined, making a show of force. With representatives of the respective states, they were greeted in the government palace by President Gutiérrez and several representatives of the diplomatic corps, who witnessed the parade from a balcony above the noisy crowd.

But underneath this dramatic show of unity, problems lingered from the outset. Within the governing organs, Villa's supporters predominated. Zapata demanded the creation of a ministry to address the agrarian question that would be entrusted to one of his partisans. The problems of reconstructing the state apparatus and organizing city administrations also arose. Many well-off families had already fled the capital, making pressing the need to control looting and the occupation of houses, and instead find tenable ways of providing for the people's basic needs.

The "terrorist" chapter of the Mexican revolution, unlike analogous experiences in other nations, seems fairly contained, mostly because Díaz's loyalists immediately left the country. Nevertheless, in the capital, some personnel from the old regime were summarily executed, including former army officers,

as well as militants accused of having collaborated with Madero and Huerta, the two principal adversaries of the respective movements. Among the most publicized cases was the assassination by Villa's men of a former journalist and apparent opponent of Díaz and Madero, who headed the Zapata delegation at Aguascalientes.

Collaboration between Villa and Zapata quickly failed at both the military and political levels.

The worker movement in the capital, furthermore, remained loyal to Carranza. In September 1912, a debating circle known as the *Casa del Obrero Mundial* was formed through the efforts of several anarchist militants; the club united the mutual aid societies with the artisan associations of the capital. While Huerta had outlawed such organizations, Obregón, in the summer of 1914, gave them a meeting place in a convent that had been requisitioned from the church. The subsequent break that arose between this organization and Zapata may be explained by cultural differences between the urban classes and the rural farmers. Villa's distance from the organization, on the other hand, was more the

*In February 1915, the* Casa del Obrero Mundial *chose sides: In exchange for greater freedom of action, the "red battalions" joined forces with Obregón's army.*

result of missed opportunities for collaboration, and his representatives' lack of success in addressing the problem of scarcities that plagued the capital.

The break with Villa would become even more profound when, in 1915, several thousand workers of the arms factories, the textile establishments, and the transport companies create "red battalions" to fight against him. Though their military role would prove insignificant, their political ties to Obregón and the Carranza movement helped shape the subsequent direction of the union movement.

In general, workers joined revolutionary groups that controlled their respective regions; this was true in the case of the railroad workers, for example. In the textile industry, territorial differences were quite marked: While the factories at Puebla suffered grave stoppages because of the lack of raw materials and continued attacks by Zapata, the plants at Orizaba and Veracruz maintained a better flow of materials, because of Carranza's control of the region. And those in the north, under Villa's dominion, were free to use the cotton produced at La Laguna.

President Gutiérrez, in the meantime, was in no condition to exercise his power from Mexico City, and conceived of the idea of instead establishing a base of support in the northeast. When he attempted to leave the city on December 26, though, he was blocked by Villa, who imprisoned him in his residence.

On January 16, 1915, in Villa's absence, Gutiérrez escaped with a military column to San Luis Potosí, bringing with him money from the general treasury. Representatives of the Convention – presided over by Roque González Garza – remained in the capital city, trying to maintain the appearance of an administration. But the looting of stores, assaults, and retaliations continued until, on January 28, under pressure from Obregón, they abandoned the city.

### Villa Returns to the North

Villa's attempt to gain control of the capital, then, was lost; neither Villa nor Zapata was capable of establishing durable alliances, and neither made the

*Strengthened by its agreement with Carranza's government, the workers' movement extended its sphere of activity and within a short time spawned union organizations in several parts of the country.*

taking of the capital a pivotal element of his policy.

For every step forward Villa took to establish himself on the national playing field, the proverbial step backward followed. After the conquest of Zacatecas, when the door was open for him to dominate the country's center, he returned to Chihuahua. Now, from the capital, he and Zapata could have followed Carranza to Veracruz; instead, he ordered his troops to return to the north. It seems that, for Villa, military considerations always won out over the political, and immediate needs dominated those of a more strategic nature. On December 10, 1914, he ordered the departure of part of his army to Torreón and the northeast, entrusting its command to General Ange-

*A detail of a Diego Rivera fresco depicting Holy Week festivities.*

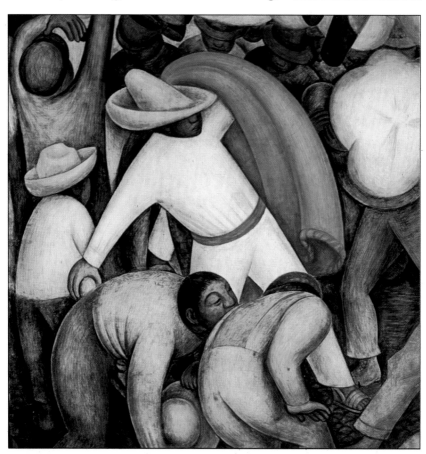

les. Villa moved in the direction of Guadalajara to oppose a force united under Carranza, in this way exposing the capital and southern regions to his adversaries.

Villa assigned great importance to the security of the border and relations with the United States. Primarily for this motive, on January 5, 1915, he headed toward Chihuahua, where clashes between Maytorena and Carranza supporters, who controlled the border zone of Naco in Sonora, flared up, creating a tense international situation.

US military representatives, in the meantime, insisted that their own government heighten vigilance along the Arizona border, primarily to prevent the Naco revolutionaries from acquiring arms and munitions,

## THE REVOLUTIONARIES IN MEXICO CITY

**F**ernando Benítez, among the most prestigious of contemporary Mexican intellectuals, writes primarily about Mexican history. Of the entrance by the popular armies into Mexico City, he writes: "By the time of General Obregón's second entry, Mexico City was under siege, attacked, and famished. Zapata's men had destroyed the aqueduct of Xochimilco, and the city lacked water. The city was short of coal, and the old trees along the streets were cut down. With the lines of communication interrupted, there was no more corn, and long lines of specters

clothed in rags formed in front of the stores.... The city's inhabitants had the chance to witness the unusual sight of wealthy merchants and shopkeepers – primarily Spanish – accused of speculation and the cornering of provisions, sweep the main streets, as they were obliged to do by the bayonets of the troops. Typhus wiped out the poor neighborhoods. There was no doubt that this was revolution – a revolution in which some were called "conventionists," others "constitutionalists," who accused one another of being reactionaries, traitors, enemies of the people; the

enormous river of farmers who entered and exited non-stop, on horse and armed to the teeth, was reduced irreconcilably to: supporters of Carranza, and supporters of Villa. The only certainty was that the old class comprising people who had been deluded by progress, and the large landowners, had been eliminated. The provisory generals had taken control of their cars and transformed their residences into seats of supreme power. ■

From: Fernando Benítez, *Lázaro Cárdenas y la Revolucion Mexicana* (Mexico City: FCE, 1977) II: 64.

and from trading freely across the border. Villa proposed himself as a mediator in this critical situation, and at El Paso, Texas, met with General Hugh Scott, a high-ranking US representative. They agreed that Maytorena should retreat south, that Naco should be evacuated and the border closed to international traffic until Mexico established a legitimate, recognizable government. Carranza and his supporters were permitted to relocate to the east, to Agua Prieta, with the guarantee that they would not be disturbed there. This accord seemed to demonstrate a fair degree of understanding between the American representatives and Villa; and for Villa, it conveyed the sense that he was the uncontested leader of the north.

In the meantime, he learned of President Gutiérrez's flight. Since his delegate retained formal responsibility for governing in the capital, Villa next established his headquarters at Aguascalientes, in an attempt to control the country's center. As commander-in-chief of the Convention's army, Villa became the primary political authority in the territories of the north and center, and on February 2, 1915 (after a renewed occupation of Mexico City on the part of Obregón) created an autonomous administration of his own divided into three branches (foreign affairs, internal affairs, and treasury), located in the city of Chihuahua.

During this phase of the revolutionary civil war, therefore, four governments claimed to represent Mexican national aspirations: Carranza, with his base at Veracruz, and three governments formed as a consequence of the Convention. These were the permanent assembly, which moved from Mexico City to Zapata's territory; the government-in-flight of Eulalio Gutiérrez, which exercised its authority in limited areas of Zacatecas and San Luis Potosí; and Villa's, in Chihuahua. Only this last, however, claimed vast territory and an effective and well-equipped army.

### Two Movements in Conflict
Military victory seemed be the only way to achieve a political solution. In early 1915, Villa appeared to

*A battalion of indigenous yaqui, fighting with bow and arrow, beside troops of the constitutionalist army. Below, la calavera (the skull), an omnipresent figure in the engravings of José Guadalupe Posada, shown here resembling a federal soldier.*

many to be the only revolutionary leader capable of victory, and therefore of imposing peace on the country. Largely responsible for disseminating this impression were newspapers, US diplomats, who, in various capacities, followed these events, and US military officials, long present along Mexico's border, who observed first hand Villa's capacity to maintain order in his own territories. Reinforcing their conviction was the sense that Carranza has been weakened. Villa also enjoyed strong popular support within his own country, since, from the time of the battle at Zacatecas in June 1914, he had quashed all forms of military resistance.

Villa's movement did not differ from Carranza's in its social or ideological foundations. Really, the movements were defined by their leaders, whose personal traits were then amplified by the personalities of the lesser bosses, who carried with them their own regionally-based popular support. Two such Villa supporters were ex-bandit Tomás Urbina and former railroad worker Rodolfo Fierro, who both stood out for their arbitrary acts of violence. The latter, in particular, became legendary for his bloody enterprises and eventual disappearance in the shifting sands of the territories north of Chihuahua.

Members of all social classes were able to find a voice within Villa's fold – from the poorest workers; to members, like the Maderos, of the upper classes; to former army officers. In fact, after the fall of Huerta, Villa welcomed anyone prepared to fight against Carranza, demonstrating tolerance toward Catholics and the church hierarchy itself. If this broad collaboration helped Villa extend his own territorial domination, nevertheless the various sympathizers remained prisoners of their recent past, and their preference for Villa's alignment rather than another often depended more on opportunism or personal rivalries than political conviction. In fact, the various revolutionary leaders had quite similar concerns regarding social policy; they all tried to enact

*Revolutionary boss Fortino Sámano, in a defiant pose, smokes his last cigar before being executed in January 1917.*

reforms, abolish "servile" forms of labor, and regulate labor policies. Villa's supporters, though, were prepared to establish a government that did not necessarily adhere to existing constitutional models, while Carranza's sympathizers preferred the tradition of constitutional liberalism, recalling their political activity as Maderistas.

In the end, Carranza won the broad support of the middle class, and his supporters showed greater aptitude acting as representatives outside of their home territories, and with the labor unions.

Early in 1915, Villa extended his dominion to the entire north, and attempted to give his movement greater political consistency. After General Angeles' conquest of the important industrial city of Monterrey, a climate of expectation set in. Villa's distanc-

*S*eated on school benches, Villa's dorados *learn to read and write.*

ing of Antonio Villareal, a constitutionalist governor who supported Carranza, was met with favor. Villareal, an old militant of the anarcho-syndicalist group of Flores Magón and candidate for the presidency at the Aguascalientes Convention, was installed as governor of the state of Nuevo Leon in April 1914, after the defeat of Huerta in the north. He initiated a policy of tight control by the public administration over industry, banks, and commerce. And in an attempt to stop sales of property favoring foreign citizens, he had formed a local agrarian commission charged with expropriating landed property, reassigning it as rental property, and establishing the amount of income to be gained.

Villarreal, like other middle-class revolutionaries of the north, was known as a fervid anti-cleric who burned confessionals in the piazza and established committees on public health. Similar events happened throughout of the country; Villa himself voiced intentions of expelling foreign clerics, especially those of Spanish origin.

But Villa's changed attitude and greater tolerance – he even tried to protect the rights of US citizens – fed expectations of a more flexible policy, and guaranteed him a broad following in the north and in important cities, such as Monterrey and Guadalajara.

Villa's later difficulties were tied to the outbreak of World War I. As his financial resources declined, the price of arms on the US market rose steadily.

## THE REVOLUTION AND ANTI-CLERICALISM

**D**uring the Maderist period, the Catholic National Party emerged and during both the political and administrative elections of 1912 met with marked success. With Huerta's rise to power, the party split – in fact dissolved – while the ecclesiastical leadership supported the new government. In the dispute between the revolutionaries and the Church, various elements became issues: the revolutionaries' emphasis on broadening public education, the radical ideas of several revolutionaries, and Catholic support of Huerta.
By 1914, anti-clericalism

became especially associated with Carranza's movement, and manifested itself in the confiscation of church buildings, forced loans, and sometimes the expulsion of foreign, mostly

Spanish, clerics. Measures limiting the church's freedom of action, especially with regard to education, were juridically sanctioned by the 1917 constitution. ■

Further, the stock of cattle on the haciendas of Chihuahua decreased from continuous sales, and cotton production in La Laguna was insufficient to satisfy the demands of the treasury. In addition, US mining interests exerted pressure to stimulate production to satisfy the war industry, and President Wilson wanted a stable political situation.

In the meantime, reasons for clashes with Carranza were plentiful. In early 1915, after Carranza consolidated his political and military forces at Veracruz and in the Yucatan peninsula, oil exports increased. For several months, Villa's brigades and Carranza's troops waged battles for control of the oil-rich region north of Veracruz and the port of Tampico. The southern half of Yucatan, once at the margins of the revolution, had a flourishing agriculture, based primarily on the production of *henequén*, a plant whose fiber is used in the manufacture of rope. This region of Mexico grew almost 100 percent of the US requirement, and its export was in the hands of Harvester International of Chicago.

*With the exceptions of northern territories controlled by Villa and those in the south under Zapata, the rest of the country was under the jurisdiction of Carranza who, after the US withdrawal, converted Veracruz into the launching pad for his offensive. At left, another of José Posada's skulls, this one wearing a woman's hat.*

As of 1914, Carranza's attempts to dominate the region had provoked both the local oligarchies and the US government. In March 1915, the determined Carranza sent Salvador Alvarado to the region, with an army of 7,000. Alvarado established a governing commission that exercised a monopoly over the sale of the fiber, determined its price, and imposed new taxes on its export, thus diverting profits from both the foreign concerns and the local oligarchies. At the same time, additional tensions with the US arose because of the difficult situation in Mexico City, a city that was home to many foreigners, but which remained without a stable government through the summer of 1915.

Further consolidation of power by Villa depended on the possibility of reaching an agreement that included a political solution with the United States, a revival of economic activity, and a more efficient use of the country's raw materials, especially with regard to the needs of the American war industry. And while pressures and hypotheses of all kinds multiplied – from people of all economic persuasions, European diplomats (especially British), US functionaries, who were at times in contact with counter-revolutionaries in the form of Mexican exiles – Wilson tried to guide the parties to an agreement. In early June, he sent a formal request to Villa and Carranza to end the civil war, but only the former was so disposed. At this point, a pan-American conference was called, to determine a plan for designating a provisory president, to whom financial aid would be awarded to rebuild the country.

When the conference met at the beginning of August, Villa found himself in serious military difficulties, and Wilson revised his Mexican policy.

*Soldiers departing for the front. The outcome of the civil war between the armies of Carranza and Obregón on one hand and those of Villa on the other remained uncertain until mid-1915.*

### The Counterattack by Obregón and Carranza

The first serious blows to Villa's military domination came in the spring and summer of 1915. Following military defeat, the administration of Chihuahua collapsed, in part because of the rapid devaluation of the currency and also because of the difficulties encountered in activating a reform program that had been too long in coming. Then, Wilson's decision to give de facto recognition to the Carranza government on October 19 opened the way to Villa's definitive political defeat.

The decisive clash between the two principal revolutionary alignments – that is, between Villa and Carranza's constitutionalists – would finally end in favor of the latter, primarily because of the superiority of Carranza's military leader, Alvaro Obregón.

In early 1915, Obregón succeeded in maintaining control of the rail lines linking Veracruz to the center of the country, despite Zapata's activity on the outskirts of the capital. He also decided to harden his attack against Villa in the plains of the state of Guanajuato, relying on logistical support from the troops behind the front. The battle lasted for three months. Two battles occurred near Celaya in April; then fighting continued for the entire month of May at León. The final battle took place at Aguascalientes in early July.

At the end of March, before the opening of this war front, Villa had ordered his brigades, which were threatening the oil-producing zone of Tampico, to retreat, thus clearing the way for Carranza's forces to enter this region.

Obregón made his stand in the city of Celaya with 11,000 men, knowing that control of this city would ensure protection of the supply route from the south.

Ignoring Angeles' counsel, Villa decided to launch an assault against Obregón at Celaya. Despite clear numerical superiority, Villa's forces were defeated.

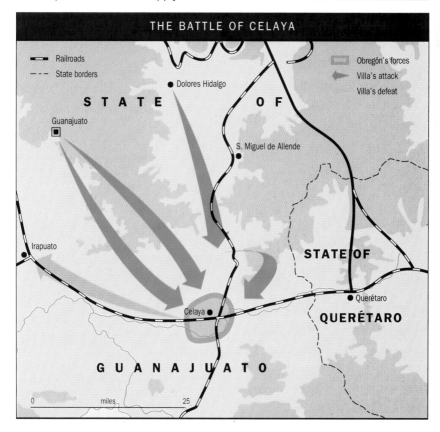

THE BATTLE OF CELAYA

Railroads
State borders

Obregón's forces
Villa's attack
Villa's defeat

S T A T E          O F

Dolores Hidalgo

Guanajuato

S. Miguel de Allende

Irapuato

STATE OF

Celaya

Querétaro

QUERÉTARO

G U A N A J U A T O

0          miles          25

General Felipe Angeles advised Villa to wait to attack until Obregón advanced northward, but Villa, then at Torreón, wanted to confront his foe immediately, convinced that he would defeat him quickly with his greater numbers. In the ensuing battles around Celaya, Villa's cavalry charges proved ineffective, and over a period of several days, the number of wounded grew to the thousands.

The psychological impact of the defeat was so great that several brigades abandoned Villa. The battles continued, and Obregón – who, in the meantime, had lost his arm and gained the nickname "the one-armed man of Celaya" – attacked Aguascalientes on July 10, forcing Villa to retreat to the north. By the end of December, Villa was pushed out of the northeast and Torreón. That city, in fact, became the stronghold for the final attack that Carranza's constitutionalists prepared to launch against Chihuahua.

In early 1915, Villa had tried to reorganize his

## OBREGÓN AT CELAYA

At Celaya in 1915, the armies of Villa and Obregón confronted one another for the first time on April 6 and 7, and then again from the 13th to the 15th. Villa's losses were great, with about 4,000 dead, among them at least 5 generals and over 100 officers; over 5,000 wounded, and 6,000 taken prisoner. Further, nearly 1,000 horses and 30 large-bore cannons fell into the hands of the constitutionalists.

Beyond the dry statistics of numbers of dead and wounded, the importance of the battle in terms of the psychology and tactics of the leaders is eloquently expressed in Martín Luis Guzmán in his novel, The

*Eagle and the Serpent* (1928). "Obregón's tactics," writes Guzman, "consisted, above all, in drawing the enemy to a particular area, and then forcing him to attack, making him lose courage and strength, and eventually dominating and destroying him at the moment when his material and moral

superiority excluded the risk of defeat. It is possible that Obregón would never have succeeded in any of the brilliant undertakings that had brought fame upon Villa: he lacked Villa's audacity and his genius.... But Obregón knew how to assemble his means and wait; he knew how to choose his battlegrounds – those sites that would place the enemy at a disadvantage, and he knew how to deliver the coup de grace to opposing forces when they were irreparably compromised. He was always on the offensive, but with defensive methods." ■

From: Martín Luis Guzmán, *Obras completas* (Mexico City: Compañia General de Ediciones, 1961) I: 366.

administration to guarantee (1) communications throughout the north, (2) the provisioning of high priority supplies, (3) the strengthening of commerce in the area, and (4) the prohibition of hoarding and speculation. Nevertheless, following the battle at Celaya, Villa's paper money began to lose its value.

With the collaboration of several experts, Villa embarked upon a project of agrarian reform that provided for the redistribution of land to farmers. Despite his agreement with Zapata's ideas for agrarian reform, which went forward undisturbed while the revolutionary groups were busy fighting in central Mexico, Villa's program did not address the problem of communal lands. Villa's project, in fact, left ample freedom to the state commissions to establish the actual mechanisms of reform, while Terraza's holdings in Chihuahua were set aside for the combatants of Villa's Northern Division. To rejuvenate mining activity, in March Villa decreed a loss of mining con-

*After the defeat at Celaya, Villa attempted to resist his adversaries' further strikes by sabotaging rail lines.*

cessions if, within a few months, mining was not resumed.

But all of these changes were restricted to paper; they arrived too late to be realized. If they showed an attempt to establish the ground for long-term administrative action, Villa, after his first military turnovers, found himself needing to come to grips with more

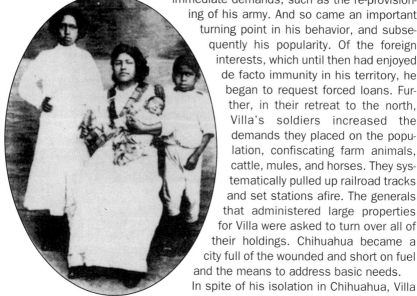

*The climate of war even disrupts familial tranquility: Here, a mother has herself photographed with her children and a cartridge around her neck.*

immediate demands, such as the re-provisioning of his army. And so came an important turning point in his behavior, and subsequently his popularity. Of the foreign interests, which until then had enjoyed de facto immunity in his territory, he began to request forced loans. Further, in their retreat to the north, Villa's soldiers increased the demands they placed on the population, confiscating farm animals, cattle, mules, and horses. They systematically pulled up railroad tracks and set stations afire. The generals that administered large properties for Villa were asked to turn over all of their holdings. Chihuahua became a city full of the wounded and short on fuel and the means to address basic needs.

In spite of his isolation in Chihuahua, Villa still had an army of 13,000, and in October he contemplated launching a counteroffensive with Maytorena's troops in Sonora, by way of the cordillera, against Carranza's men in Agua Prieta. If they succeeded, he would control the entire western frontier; then he could move on to the south, via the coast, to take Guadalajara with his Durango allies, and renew the alliance with Zapata in the center. But this plan soon revealed itself to be too ambitious.

### Villa's Army at the End

The element that most directly contributed to Villa's military failure originated on the diplomatic front, when the United States recognized Carranza's provisory government in Veracruz on October 19. This decision, contested by oil-producing interests, was made by Wilson and his close collaborators in the face of their inability to determine who among the contenders might emerge as the politically most viable candidate. Wilson believed a quick decision would check the dangers that might otherwise have led to a further delay or direct intervention and the subsequent imposition of a conservative government.

The First World War made Wilson wish to avoid any traumatic solution to the Mexican crisis. Even if Carranza, who controlled much of the national territory, was not the choice of American and British oil companies, Wilson's primary concern was to halt interference by the Europeans in Mexico.

Germany had begun blocking American arms shipments with its submarine fleet, hoping to impede US entry into the conflict on the side of its European allies. Germany hoped to provoke armed conflict between Mexico and the US by manipulating conservative Mexican groups in exile, instigating skirmishes and provocations in the border zones, and feeding the fears of US oil companies with regard to the policies of Carranza. A war between the two nations, in fact, would have hindered Mexican oil production and slowed oil shipments to England.

All of this weighed heavily to influence Wilson to give conditional support to Carranza, an action that signified the definitive abandonment of any hope for

*Hunger and misery struck many areas. In this drawing, the common people are depicted as a skeletal dog who, standing before a ruined factory, witnesses the "flight" of basic goods.*

## VILLA'S AGRARIAN LAW

On May 24, 1915, after his first major encounters with the forces of Alvaro Obregón, Villa issued an agrarian reform decree from León, in Guanajuato. Its major points included:

"**Art. 1**. Large landholdings are considered to be incompatible with the peace and prosperity of the republic. Thus, the state governments, during the first three months after the issuance of this law, will set the maximum size limits of which a single person may be the proprietor within that state; no one will be permitted to possess or acquire land with a surface area exceeding that established....
**Art. 2**. ...The government of

every state will review all of the specificities within its jurisdiction, the volume of irrigation, the population density, the quality of the earth, the amount actually under cultivation, and every

other element that might serve to determine the limit beyond which a large property might become a threat to institutional stability or social equilibrium." ■

US support for Villa's movement.

As a first act of goodwill, on November 1, Wilson consented to the passage of 3,000 of Carranza's men through US territory to reinforce the stronghold of Agua Prieta in Sonora, which was by then under siege by Villa. Wilson's action enabled Carranza's reinforcements to deflect Maytorena, who had been supporting Villa. Betrayed by the US, Villa, in response, imposed charges on the American companies involved in mining in the Sonora; he sequestered their silver, and began to sack Chihuahua's Mormon colonies, to whom he had earlier guaranteed non-interference.

By the end of 1915, Villa's entire movement began to collapse. His Durango allies were defeated, and some deserted their positions when Carranza promised amnesty if they lay down their arms. Villa himself was declared an outlaw. On December 20, his lieutenants at Ciudad Juárez surrendered, and

*In this political cartoon, the US is beset by annoying international problems: Both war in Europe and revolution in Mexico disturb the sleep of Uncle Sam.*

Villa, from the government palace at Chihuahua, realized that his military campaign had to end. He released his men to their prior occupations, and his army dissolved. Two days later, Carranza's troops entered the state capital.

Many of Villa's officers and soldiers surrendered their arms, but some began guerrilla actions. The amnesty decreed by Carranza was not extended to Villa's political advisers, nor to sympathizers and collaborators with the Villa regime, and thus, many were forced into exile. These civilian supporters became victims of the change in government, excluded from public life for the duration of Carranza's rule.

The world of Mexican exiles in American border cities became, not surprisingly, quite complex, composed as it was of people who had fought in various situations and dreamed of personal revenge. There were the ex-federalists, Huerta's supporters, Orozco's men, and finally Villa's supporters. Many attempts were made to transform the frontier into a source of permanent conflict between the two governments, and there were no shortage of plots involving agents generally, in one form or another, tied to Germany.

Villa organized a guerrilla movement in the mountainous regions of Chihuahua and Durango, allying himself even with the old rebels – insurgents of the Madero epoch who had later joined up with Orozco and Huerta, and against whom Villa himself had once fought. Villa expressed his political resentment at this point against US interests in northern Mexico, systematically demanding money and inflicting damage with shows of force and spontaneous attacks.

Villa's response was not born of his natural instinct for rebellion, as some would have it, but rather, of the political defeat of his movement and his conviction that he was betrayed. Villa's anti-Americanism and Carranza's inability to stop him would spawn strong conflicts between the United States and Mexico, especially during the early months of 1916.

The two nations did not come to actual war, but relations between Carranza, the United States, and the European powers became ever more complex. And Pancho Villa would not go away.

*On the Mexico–US border there thrived a complex world of exiles adept at exploiting disagreements between the two nations.*

# Chapter 5

# THE VICTORS AND THE VANQUISHED

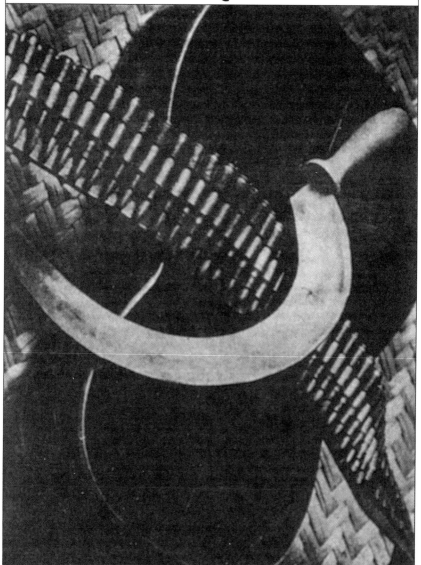

By 1916 Mexico was on the brink of dissolution. Villa played his last card – as a guerrilla. But in January 1917, Carranza's supremacy was clinched by the ratification of the constitution, which opened a new phase of economic and social development in the country.

Beginning in 1915, Villa's behavior was shaped by his mistaken conviction that a secret pact reinforcing American economic and political influence in Mexico had been reached between the United States and Carranza.

The search for a political solution led, over the course of the next year, to the development of several plans that were true conspiracies sponsored by pressure groups and high-ranking officers of the US State Department, in collaboration with leaders of American finance and conservative Mexican exiles. Their aim was to install a government that would make Mexico a virtual American protectorate. Villa attributes Wilson's changed attitude in his dealings with Carranza to two factors: the breadth of the concessions granted Carranza in exchange for his authorization of American troop movements through Texas territory into Sonora, and a presumed US loan to Carranza.

In effect, Villa, who had been the object of similar offers during the preceding months, believed that Carranza had made a clandestine agreement. Villa, in an early November manifesto revealed, with abundant details that have been shown to be unsupported

*Tina Modotti's photograph portrays the symbols of Mexico's revolutionary epic: the sickle, the bullet cartridge, and the guitar.*

*The Carranza government rejected every US attempt to violate Mexico's sovereignty.*

by fact, Carranza's secret deal. With this manifesto, Villa challenged Carranza to fight, in the name of national independence.

Without his army, and without a solid territorial base, Villa attempted to break the alliance between Wilson and Carranza, and to provoke the fall of the latter by attacking US interests in Mexico. As a consequence of this new strategy, in early 1916, Villa occupied a large estate in Chihuahua belonging to William Randolph Hearst, the American press baron, and ordered the execution of seventeen engineers who had arrived in Mexico to start repair operations in several mines.

But the episode that had the most domestic and international repercussions was Villa's attack, at the head of 500 men at dawn on March 9, on the military garrison of the small American city of Columbus, New Mexico, a couple miles from the border. The occupation lasted several hours and concluded with the burning of several buildings and more than 100 dead on both sides.

### The Guerrilla Movement Spreads

The invasion of Columbus reinforced the arguments of those in the US who had long favored direct Mexican intervention. Wilson decided to send in a military contingent to chase Villa, after requesting authorization to do so from Carranza. Despite Carranza's denial of this request, on March 15, more than 5,000 men under the command of General Pershing entered the state of

Chihuahua with the goal of squashing the guerrilla movement and capturing Villa. Neither objective was realized. Villa succeeded in undermining relations between Carranza and the US, even though his action did not lead to the war between the two nations that many observers expected. With his arms shipments blocked, Carranza tried to obtain loans from Japan and Germany, in exchange for favoring anti-American economic and diplomatic policies.

The "punitive expedition" led by General Pershing pushed initially toward the interior of the Chihuahuan state. By April, several contingents arrived in the southern Chihuahuan city of Parral, where the hostility of the civilian population forced Pershing to retreat to northern Chihuahua. He set up his headquarters at Colonia Dublan, a Mormon settlement, while Carranza requested an unconditional withdrawal of American troops. In the meantime, Villa, who was moving freely through the southern part of the state, gained enormous popularity because he appeared to be the only one who would fight the invaders. Carranza limited himself to repeating the diplomatic request for US withdrawal. For Chihuahua, which had seen years of tranquility, the specter of civil war finally loomed. Villa made an appeal to patriotism, and tried to mobilize the villages against the invaders.

*A newspaper of the era carries Carranza's declaration of a nation's right to conduct its own affairs without external interference as General Pershing's US troops invade the state of Chihuahua. At left, the encampment of US forces.*

In mid-September of 1916, Villa occupied the city of Chihuahua for several hours, freeing prisoners and rounding up provisions; he reoccupied it in November, and then, by the end of December, was installed in the city of Torreón for ten days. In Torreón, he was able to re-create an army of 10,000, but in early 1917, he was again defeated.

To impede the expansion of the guerrilla movement, Carranza encouraged the formation of local civilian militias, which were not under the command of the new constituitionalist army, and which, in Chihuahua, seemed to have a certain capacity to unite the population, renewing the political strength of some sectors. Carranza's firmness regarding the withdrawal of American troops, and his neutrality in the world conflict, accompanied by his overtures toward Germany, fueled new plans for revenge on the part of US interest groups.

At the same time, Mexico's general insecurity and economic difficulties (inflation, paralysis of production, and famine) accentuated internal divisions. In addition to Villa's guerrillas, analogous movements spread throughout the country; even though they did not represent a viable political alternative, they proved themselves to be very strong locally. With the virtual disappearance of the government of the 1915 convention, Carranza launched a military campaign to re-take control of the rural districts surrounding Mexico City.

In Morelos, where Zapata had effected agrarian reform, the great popular movement broke down into small groups that maintained an active presence, and for several years resisted the Carranza government's efforts to control the region. Only after Zapata's assassination in an ambush, on April 10, 1919, would an accord be reached with the leaders of the movement.

## THE PUNITIVE EXPEDITION

In March 1916, 5,000 men entered Mexico under the command of US General Pershing. By the time of their withdrawal in January 1917, they would number 25,000. In April 1916, Obregón, as Carranza's war minister, went to El Paso, Texas, and met unsuccessfully with US representative Hugh Scott in an attempt to find a solution. In the meantime, Carranza ordered his troops in the state of Chihuahua to impede the movement of US troops. On June 21, a battle broke out between the two sides near Carrizal; 8 Americans and 50 Mexicans died. Carranza took and returned 23 prisoners, after stripping them of their ordnance. A meeting between representatives of the two governments in Atlantic City established the protocol for US troop withdrawal and international border controls. But the situation remained stagnant until January 22, 1917, when the withdrawal of the troops began; it was complete by February 5. ■

In several parts of the state of Sonora, central Mexico, and San Luis Potosí, the guerrillas concentrated in predominantly indigenous areas, where the seizure of land produced strong expressions of revenge. In other areas, widespread banditry erupted for reasons of mere survival, a phenomenon that generally involved small groups of men, numbering several hundred, that led raids and similar disturbances, and then found refuge in the mountains.

In the oil-producing regions of Veracruz, the guerrillas were financed directly by US corporations that exerted pressure on Carranza's political economy for the duration of the world war. In 1916, a number of US groups with interests in Mexico actually gave their support to the nephew of Porfirio Díaz, who, with the help of former officers of the old federal army, tried to transform the guerrilla movements in the southern states into a liberation army.

The year 1916, then, was not only a year of famine, but more than anything else, a year in which the country found itself on the edge of dissolution.

In 1917, though, the situation changed profoundly. On January 31, a new constitution was drafted, elections held in March, and on May 1, Carranza assumed the presidency. Following Wilson's decision to intervene in the world war, in early February 1917, Washington pulled its military contingent out of Chihuahua. At the same time, the US government recognized the new Carranza government, and on April 2, declared war on Germany. Both events reduced external pressures on Mexico.

The role of the United States in Mexican affairs remained open, however. Another serious crisis came in mid-1919, after the end of the world war. US oil companies, fearing the conse-

*General Pershing at his tent. The "punitive expedition," undertaken to capture Villa in March 1916, after the Mexican leader's foray across the border and burning of the city of Columbus, failed to fulfill its mission.*

*The multiplication of guerrillas and banditry in the countryside created serious difficulties for the Carranza government.*

quences of the new constitution, opposed the price increases for crude oil that Carranza had announced. The sequester by rebel bands of American consul William Jenkins at Puebla in October 1919 and Carranza's subsequent accusations that Jenkins had been in league with the kidnappers, offered the US a new pretext for attacking Carranza.

Though in the end there was no war between the US and Mexico, even the threat of war, not to mention the political support given to internal opposition groups, destabilized the country. At the end of 1918, in fact, Mexican exiles in the US began to mobilize again, with the support of some of the local press. The exiles wanted to unify the various guerrillas, and provoke the fall of Carranza's constitutional government.

In this context, in December of 1918, General Felipe Angeles decided to re-enter Chihuahua to verify a pact with Villa. After several months of preparation, between April and June of 1919, Angeles and Villa attacked Parral, Chihuahua, and Ciudad Juárez, but failed to obtain the popular support they expected, despite appeals for desertion among the local militia. Villa was forced to pull back to the Durango mountains, and in November, Angeles was taken prisoner, tried by a war council, and executed.

Villa avoided capture with his relentless movement, but nevertheless, his guerrilla movement lost steam, and became marginalized. By then, the domestic and international political climates had changed, and the opposition to Carranza no longer depended exclusively on external alliances (though it continued to receive support from strong international backers); instead, support came from the Mexican workers' movement, which had been growing ever more autonomous.

### The Constitution of 1917

The constitution of 1917 was the written expression of Carranza's political alliance; it sanctioned, juridically and institutionally, the changes introduced by the revolution.

At Veracruz, Carranza had redefined his political

and social program, but his principal objective had remained the return to constitutional legality. By the spring of 1916, he had relocated to Mexico City, and there he held elections for a constituent assembly that would meet at Querétaro, between November 20, 1916, and January 31, 1917. This was an elected assembly, quite different from the convention of armed citizens held at Aguascalientes in 1914.

Carranza announced the elections by decree, proclaiming the freedom to vote and universal suffrage – though excluding collaborators of the various other "governments" and opponents of Carranza. Supporters of Villa, Zapata, and the governments of the Convention, as well as advocates of the old regimes of Díaz or Huerta, were not allowed to run for the constituent congress. Participation remained below 30 percent of those eligible to vote, in some districts failing to reach even 10 percent. Although it was difficult to establish the propriety of the elections – Chihuahua, for example, was involved in a full-blown civil war – the regulatory "commission of the powers of the constituent assembly" accepted the credentials of 218 of the 240 deputies to be elected.

Given these conditions, the delegates of Querétaro were basically Carranza's supporters. One-quarter had completed university studies (they were lawyers, engineers, doctors, teachers, and journalists), while others were artisans, foremen, or simply combatants. Absent from these last were the principal commanders of the constitutionalist army, beginning with Obregón himself. Some deputies had been

*E*miliano Zapata portrayed as a martyr in a Diego Rivera fresco.

active in the political life of the Maderist period, or in the fight against Huerta, while others had distinguished themselves as military leaders. Nevertheless, the assembly represented a broad range of political positions, from moderate to radical. Though there was no well-defined ideological cohesion, the delegates were united in their aversion toward landowners and foreign capitalists, and their defense of liberty and social justice. The Liberal Constitutionalist Party, which formed in 1916 to support Carranza, was nothing more than an electoral instrument; it did not unite the various currents around a concrete political program.

On December 1, 1916, at the assembly of Querétaro, Carranza presented a constitutional project. After years of civil war, his intention was to give the historic arrangement new life based in the liberal tradition, favorable to social progress, and respecting of individual and collective freedom. The proposed text followed the 1857 constitution, with modifications regarding term limits for the president of the republic and state governors, the suppression of the vice presidency, and the introduction of direct suffrage.

The deputies unanimously supported nationalism in economic matters and the tabling of discussion of

*A textile factory in the capital, employing exclusively women, at the turn of the century. The support organized labor gave Carranza in the cities proved decisive.*

all forms of parliament. In this, the idea prevailed of maintaining, even reinforcing, a strong executive branch headed by a strong president.

The 1917 constitution laid out principles guaranteeing individual rights and abolishing every form of servility. Certain articles provoked debate and at times were rewritten entirely. Some aggravated the church by placing limitations on religious orders with regard to instructional materials and the right to possess goods. Monastic orders were abolished and religious ceremonies outside of the church forbidden. The application of these provisions raised strong protest almost immediately, and were to become even more divisive during the late 1920s. The constitution's most innovative articles were those relating to the social function of property (Article 27) and the regulation of labor (Article 123).

Article 27, in particular, which had to be entirely rewritten, states in its final form that the land, water, and products of a given locale belong "originally to the nation," a formulation aligned with the classic liberal conception of property. Therefore, the article sanctions the right of expropriation with indemnity, in the best interests of the public. This notion would hold great importance in delineating

*With the 1917 constitution, the political and social upheaval created by the revolution was redirected into a clear juridical path.*

**A**rnaldo Córdova, scholar of political thought of the revolutionary period, writes the following about the Mexican revolution of 1917: "The ancient privileges brought on the disintegration by fostering an inevitable rivalry between the various components of the society;

at the service of all of its components.

"Liberal Democracy, which in Europe had been affirmed by forces that existed before the development of the nation-state, had no role in Mexico; here, one did not think of placing restraints on the actions of the state, since its function required just the

27, which addressed the social function of property. Pastor Rouaix, governor of Durango in 1913, close collaborator of Venustiano Carranza and president of the commission that prepared Article 27, recalled: "The fundamental proposal of the delegates of Querétaro, which conveyed the unanimous sentiment of all of the revolutionaries, was that, in Mexican legislation, the basic right to property of the society should be held above that of the individual, so that its distribution, use and productivity might better be regulated.

"This principle, conceived in a nebulous form during the early phases of the revolution, guided the successive evolution of ideas and debate, since it was clear that, without it, the blood spilled, the wealth destroyed, and the sacrifice for the country, would have been in vain, since no reform would be possible.

social groups that might have worked together were transformed into enemies, and this provoked a significant slowdown in the development of the country, which had not been able to exploit its own natural and human resources, and had been slave to a parasitory and non-productive elite.

"The government's job, therefore, consisted of rebuilding the unity of Mexican society, reconciling sectors that had become adversaries, and placing itself

opposite…. The Constitution of 1917 symbolically represented all classes and all interests: it was the symbol of a democracy of coalition, in which all classes participated – except members of the old privileged classes who were not prepared to renounce their privileges, and obviously, large landowners, since the Constitution had declared itself to be expressly against this group."

Among the elements of the new constitution that aroused substantial debate was Article

"The promises… would have fallen irremediably before the first appeal of any judge after the return of constitutional order, vociferously pointing out the failure of the revolution. Thus, our first priority in this our first article was the explicit declaration that the ownership of lands and water included within the national confines was above all the nation's, and that the nation had the right to transfer possession directly to small landowners, thereby creating private property." ∎

the central ideas of subsequent agrarian reform.

At the origin of Article 27 lay the conviction that the principal cause of malaise in the rural areas was the indigenous communities' loss of communal lands, and that the agrarian problem had to be resolved by dividing up the large landholdings and providing support to small property owners. The revolutionary leaders had acted everywhere to limit individual rights to property in the name of the collective good, a principle implicit in the various decrees released during the armed phase. The new constitutional article introduced a general juridical norm that rendered effective the constitutive right to private property, but only according to the limits imposed by society.

The deputies envisioned the restitution of communal lands (those lands to which the single communities claimed ancient rights – occasionally, documents existed that concretely demonstrated ancient possession) and the assignment of new lands as necessary to guarantee the survival of components of rural communities. In reality, the distribution of lands was quite minimal until 1920; Carranza, himself, relinquished haciendas and confiscated goods. For the short term, proposed concessions of land were sometimes even annulled in favor of foreign citizens.

*Carranza visits a military uniform factory in 1918, a year after the translation of his political project into a new constitution. At left, members of the commission that drew up Article 27, presided over by Pastor Rouaix.*

In most places (except Morelos and several surrounding areas), the hacienda survived as a productive unit. This phenomenon was unusual when compared to other revolutions; the situation evolved because Villa and Carranza, during the armed period, had relied on administering haciendas to finance their movements. Now Carranza returned these holdings to their legitimate owners, in return for an explicit and formal renunciation of indemnification of the damage suffered during the revolution. Luis Terrazas, for example, invoked the restitution of his holdings in Chihuahua, and in March 1919, Carranza accepted his request. But though the landowners gained back their land, they were defeated politically, since they were no longer eligible to represent the landowning class at either the local or the national level.

*An engraving from the time of a "red soldier" – a union member who joined Carranza's forces.*

Article 123 of the constitution established a general framework for protecting the rights of workers and labor unions; this was the fruit of the presence of many representatives of labor unions among those gathered at the Querétaro assembly. The delegates created a modern work code that included regulations requiring an eight-hour work day, the defense of women's working rights (salary parity, maternity protection), protection of children, firing only for just cause, a minimum wage, the right to instruction, and assistance for illnesses. At the same time, all forms of servile work were abolished in the countryside, freeing the workers from old and burdensome obligations. The obligation to provide a monetary salary in the countryside was introduced for the first time.

The ambiguities left by the new constitution would emerge in the course of social protests: requests to legalize strikes began and state "conciliation commissions" to arbitrate labor conflicts were introduced.

The right to strike was recognized only if the expressed intent was to reach harmony between the classes. Later experience was to demonstrate that the margins of interpretation turned out to be too broad, since the legality of a strike depended on the possibility of stipulating binding contracts between the workers and the owners. In the arbitration commissions, the public employees assigned to perform such tasks had broad discretionary powers to induce the entrepreneurs and union representatives to come together; the power of the arbitrator thus had the potential to become a political weapon in the hands of government representatives, as the arbitrator could easily tilt the outcome either way.

After the constitution was hammered out, a disagreement with the oil-producing companies immediately surfaced, with legal, fiscal and international repercussions. In the decade from 1910 to 1920, Mexico's annual production of petroleum went from 3.5 million to 157 million barrels, a figure that accounted for 20 percent of global production. While his radical supporters wanted to nationalize the foreign companies and apply the constitutional dictates retroactively, Carranza, attempting to avoid a head-on confrontation with the United States, interpreted Article 27 less restrictively, applying it only to future agreements.

But though Carranza did not modify the nature of the rights already granted the foreign corporations, he still tried to limit the easements and fiscal privileges they enjoyed. In April 1917, he introduced new taxes on production, and in February 1918, extended them to lands not yet in production, obligating the companies to request preventive authorization for new drilling. These actions constituted the most serious affront to the US by Mexico since the onset of the revolution. Carranza deferred the strict enforcement of these new laws, but without revoking them. His aim was to keep avenues of communication open, but still defend the principle that when a nation's laws mirror its legitimate order, foreign imperialists may not change them. This realpolitik defense of national interests became one of the most enduring aspects of what has been called the "Carranza Doctrine." Oil, though, would remain a point of friction between the two nations for several decades.

*The state should regulate private property, protect the rights of the workers, and nationalize natural resources: These are the pillars of the 1917 constitution.*

# Chapter 6

# **T**HE **F**OUNDATIONS
# OF A **N**EW **M**EXICO

RECONSTRUCTION BEGAN IN THIS COUNTRY DEVASTATED BY
CIVIL WAR, AND THE LEADERSHIP, NEWLY EMERGED FROM THE
REVOLUTION, LAID THE GROUNDWORK FOR THE SOCIAL AND
ECONOMIC SYSTEM OF CONTEMPORARY MEXICO. BUT THE
POLITICAL VENDETTAS DID NOT END: CARRANZA WOULD BE
ASSASSINATED IN 1920, AND VILLA, THREE YEARS LATER.

How to return to political normalcy after three years of civil war? Carranza wanted to base government action on the primacy of law and institutions, but without a party system to help, he was overburdened fending off the weighty presence of the military revolutionary heads. These men maintained their ties to the rural masses, who were beginning to discover that the union movement, which had started to act and speak as a single entity, might not be an adequate base of support for addressing their needs.

*With the demobilization of the guerrilla formations, Villa retired to private life at his hacienda in the state of Durango. In 1923, he would fall victim to an ambush.*

The new political stability depended on the new governors' capacities to control the economic crisis and at the same time address social aspirations and expectations of change.

Agricultural production, during the years of revolution, had suffered seriously because of a regional distribution system that had been gradually changing. In 1915, in the central Mexico that was then the theater of battle between Villa and Obregón, grain cultivation had collapsed, though this was not true in Morelos, where Zapata's agrarian reform had permitted a resurgence of corn and vegetable production, nor was it true in the Yucatan, in the southern regions in general, or in the cotton-growing region of La Laguna.

But by 1916, both Morelos and Chihuahua felt the devastating effects of the guerrillas. While mining production had been paralyzed between 1914 and 1915, activity in the oil-producing regions had increased. Foundries had been closed as of 1913 or 1914, while the textile industry had witnessed ups and downs, depending on the location. In general, there was a scattered slowdown of productivity.

At this point, the conditions of the rail network were dismal because of the destruction of tracks and the shortages of locomotives and freight; this of course had grave consequences for internal commerce and the provisioning of basic needs to the large urban centers.

*The most urgent problem that the Carranza government had to confront was the shortage of basic goods, after years of violence and destruction.*

But the most immediate economic problem was that of money. During the two-year period following 1913, 200 different currencies had been placed in circulation. This kind of monetary chaos interfered with economic life – exchanges, salary policies, and price controls – so much that, by the end of 1915, the prices of basic necessities in the capital had increased by 2000 percent. As soon as Carranza gained control of a large part of the country in spring of 1916, he outlawed his adversaries' paper money, gradually substituting his own notes for those issued by others. These new notes, printed expressly for Carranza's government, were known as *infalsificables,* and were guaranteed by the gold reserves of the few banks that were still active, banks that the government had confiscated to finance the internal debt that had been growing since the revolution. Further, Carranza decided not to repay foreign debts that had been contracted (primarily with European nations) before 1913. In February 1919, under the aegis of the US company Morgan, a committee of bankers was assembled to manage the Europeans' and Americans' interests in Mexico, and to request payment for damages caused to foreigners during the revolution.

### New Political Alliances

With the return to monetary normalcy, Carranza proposed to assess purchasing power and what constituted a living wage. The economic situation seemed particularly bleak in the capital, where, a first wave of strikes hit at the end of July 1916. The strategy of the Casa del Obrero Mundial, which was based on direct action and the general strikes, lost ground within the new institutional framework. Several directors, appealing to the political authorities, adopted more flexible positions. Fearing the threat of not being able to control workers' protests, union strategists used the legal process of mediation contained in Article 123 of the constitution to persuade industrialists to reach an accord with the other side. Luis Morones, an industrial electrical worker and member of the group of anarchists that had started the Casa del Obrero Mundial, sensed the need for a broader organization of workers at the national level. Strikes followed in 1917 and 1918, and there were

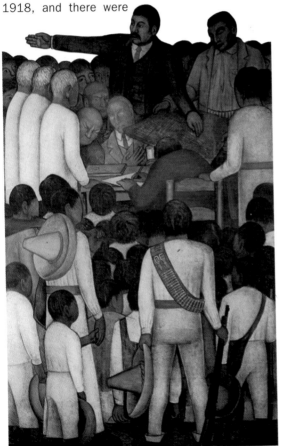

*The concession of land to the peasant farmers was one consequence of the revolution, portrayed here by Diego Rivera in a fresco of the distribution of ejidos, the parcels of land designated for collective use.*

many attempts to create a union confederation. In May 1918, a congress was convened at Saltillo, in which 120 delegates, representing over 100 associations with 7,000 affiliates, participated. This congress founded the Confederación Regional Obrera Mexicana, electing Morones secretary general. This autonomous Mexican union proposed an end to every form of passive subordination in the worker movement, and signaled an important change in the national landscape; an alliance with the Confederación became one of the requirements of holding power in the new political system.

In the elections of 1918, Carranza's supporters won a majority, but in the later presidential elections, a coalition formed around Alvaro Obregón, who, after the installation of Carranza as constitutional president in May of 1917, had retired to private life. Obregón counted on a strong electoral base in Sonora, where, following the defeat of Villa and Maytorena at the end of 1915, the local governors had adopted a series of measures favoring the stimulation of the state economy.

In June 1919, Obregón launched his candidacy for the presidency, with the aim of unifying the forces that had fought during the revolution in a great "liberal

## THE FIRST LABOR UNION

**T**he Confederación Regional Obrera Mexicana, founded at Saltillo in 1918, became the basis for the first modern labor union. A decade later, it reached the climax of its organizational capacity, with about two million members; during the 1930s, the union movement split and reorganized anew. When the Confederación began, the strongest group within it was the miners. In June 1919, the federation of unions in the capital joined, and by 1920, it already represented some 50,000 workers. During the course of 1919, relations between workers and the Carranza government worsened because of widespread strikes undertaken for higher wages. At the end of the year, Morones and the union leadership founded the Labor Party in order to give greater political cohesion to the workers' movement. In the next year's presidential elections, the new party was instrumental in organizing Obregón's campaign. ■

*A group of Mexico City workers in an image from the early 1920s. The union movement, with Luis Morones (at left) at its head, was an important protagonist in the new alliance that led the post-revolutionary nation.*

party." Carranza, who doubted Obregón's gifts as a political leader, tried to block him. To undermine Obregón's support, Carranza interfered in the internal affairs of the state of Sonora, which provoked unanimous outcry from local leaders. In February 1920, Carranza's original party assembled and decided to support Obregón; Carranza, then, orchestrated the nomination of his own candidate to the presidency – a loyal, but obscure collaborator, whose lack of accomplishment only fortified Obregón's prestige.

On April 23, 1920, the governor of Sonora, Adolfo de la Huerta, launched what would be his last successful military campaign; he released a proclamation, the Plan of Agua Prieta, in which he accused Carranza of being unresponsive to the popular vote and of violating the sovereignty of the states. The Plan had the support of Obregón's followers and the rest of a heterogeneous and vast front of opposition to Carranza. For his part, Carranza left the capital on April 29, considering transferring his government again to Veracruz. Abandoned by the army and without sufficient means, he was forced to interrupt his voyage in the mountainous zone of Puebla, where on May 20, he was killed by a traitor at Tlaxcalantongo. A few days later, the congress elected Adolfo de la Huerta provisional president, with the charge of guaranteeing regular elections on September 5.

Obregón, who won that election with a huge majority, embodied a revolutionary boss who seemed to be a

## THE END OF CARRANZA

**F**ernando Benítez writes of Carranza's last moments in office, "The president did not surrender to reality, as he had not surrendered previously. The elderly, in their tendency to dwell on the past, try to repeat actions that, once and in other circumstances, had brought them success, and this was true in the cases of Porfirio Díaz and Venustiano Carranza. Instead of giving up, of resigning – the equivalent of suicide – he tried again to find refuge in Veracruz, and from there, protected by the forces of General Guadalupe Sanchez and his son-in-law, General Candido Aguilar, fought the rebels....

"The government took refuge in the President's sumptuous Tren Dorado. Carranza, with his dark glasses, white beard, and Texas hat, appeared as he had in 1915, surrounded by ministers and generals, always solemn and passive. From the train windows, one would see the same landscape of scorched hills, gray earth, haciendas and clay hovels. The revolution, in ten years, had advanced as slowly as his caravan, weakened by betrayals, the lack of water, and petroleum....

"This is a circular story, and troublingly so: the success of Juárez, defeated by Díaz's rebellion, Díaz in turn is defeated by Madero's rebellion; Madero is assassinated in Huerta's rebellion, Carranza is defeated by the revolution that he, himself, had led seven years earlier. Perhaps his time had come, and he was rebelling against this destiny, trying with all his force to escape the trap." ■

From Fernando Benítez, *Lázaro Cárdenas y la Revolución Mexicana* (Mexico City: FCE, 1977) II: 115–16.

guarantor of the aspirations of the people rather than those of the party. His background and reputation enabled him to consolidate his forces, like a national leader. Obregón, for example, concluded a "secret pact" in mid-1919 (it only came to light years later) with Morones and the union movement: in exchange for electoral support, Obregón would attempt to establish a ministry of labor, to be headed by an individual approved by the labor union confederation.

The terms of the social/political alliance had changed. During the armed phase, the old dominant classes were excluded from political power and forced to support conspirators or guerrillas, thus placing themselves outside of the law; the masses of farmers, while integrated into the army, had been deprived of natural leaders with political influence. The worker movement, on the other hand, had come together in the climate of a summit alliance, with the new political leaders. Setting aside his own political ideas, Obregón was alone among the revolutionary leaders in being able to perform the role of a go-between, combining the need to build a new political order with that of fueling popular hopes for meaningful social change.

### Villa and the Revolution

After 1915, Villa, who had been marginalized during this political reorganization, was the victim of unforeseen changes. The natural head of a broad popular movement, he longed for another military victory, but remained beholden to outside support – that from the US, which eventually failed him. During the five months of Adolfo de la Huerta's presidency in 1920, a general pacification reigned in the country, and the guerrilla formations were demobilized. The leaders of the Zapata movement, which had by then virtually disappeared, supported the rebellion in Sonora against Carranza, and were incorporated in the national army; the guerrilla movement in the oil-producing zone dissolved, and rebels of various persuasions surrendered spontaneously, or were forced to do so.

A problem of some significance emerged in the south in the person of the nephew of Porfirio Díaz, who maintained an important military presence, even though his

*After breaking his old alliance with Obregón, Carranza was killed in an ambush in 1920. At left, a portrait of Carranza aboard his famous Tren Dorado. Above, an engraving by Posada.*

*After laying down their arms, Pancho Villa and his personal guards devoted themselves to farming at the Canutillo hacienda.*

counter-revolutionary political positions, and his old compromise with Huerta, forced him into exile. Several of Carranza's supporters demonstrated their prudence, and removed themselves from the scene, as did many state governors.

In its dealings with Villa, who has been surrounded for months at Chihuahua, the new government initially maintained the same hostile attitude that Carranza had. In July 1920, Villa wrote a letter to Adolfo de la Huerta, in which he expressed his desire to reach an accord in exchange for his retirement to civilian life. The government agreed to give him the hacienda at Canutillo, north of Durango, near Parral, where he could dedicate himself to farming with his men; he was guaranteed a

personal escort, and given a monetary advance worth one year's agricultural expenses. Villa thus became a country gentleman, surrounded by his *dorados*; he cultivated the abandoned lands of Canutillo, constructed a school, and established a flourishing village. He lived tranquilly there with his children and new wife, Austreberta Rentería, whom he married in 1921.

With the pacification of the country, an era drew to a close. The groundwork had been laid for a new political order. But the battles of the recent past left some matters unresolved. Villa's foes continued to contemplate revenge. Obregón's main difficulties in the postwar international climate were the country's relations with the United States; in particular, the application of Article 27, having to do with oil company concessions

*O*n July 20, 1923, Pancho Villa, shown here in a photograph taken at Canutillo, fell victim to an ambush planned by Jesús Salas Barraza (on the right page).

and the payment of the foreign debt. Both questions postponed recognition of his government by the US administration. Adolfo de la Huerta, who became the minister of finance in June 1922, signed an accord with Washington that provided for payment of the foreign debt, but in exchange, secured neither new loans, nor the recognition of Obregón. In April 1923, a conference held behind closed doors in Mexico City, between personal delegations of the presidents of the two nations, resulted in a secret agreement: in exchange for the non-application of the expropriation measures mandated by Article 27 and the creation of a commission charged with quantifying the damage caused to foreign citizens by the revolution, the US government would endeavor to recognize Obregón. De la Huerta then accused Obregón of betrayal, and began to hatch a military rebellion that erupted, without success, at the year's end.

Villa, who enjoyed the sympathies of the lower classes in the north, was held up by the press as a probable candidate for governor of Durango, despite his repeated denials. In this way, fear took hold that he might align himself with Adolfo de la Huerta. And so it was that his assassination that year could be traced to the national crisis.

In July of 1923, Villa went to a place near Parral to witness the baptism of the son of one of his friends. On the morning of July 20, while driving away from Parral in a brightly colored Dodge with a few of his men as escorts, he was the victim of an ambush. The following day he was buried without military honors, but grieved by a large crowd of onlookers. Those responsible were identified as members of the army; Jesús Salas Barraza, a deputy in the Durango congress, was indicted and later jailed for his plotting of the crime. Villa's assassination was a fate that none of the great protagonists of the revolution would be able to escape; Obregón, too, was to be assassinated in 1928. In 1926, Villa's tomb was violated and his head stolen. Several decades passed before his name was sculpted in the Chamber of Deputies, and only in 1969 was an equestrian statue erected to him in Mexico City.

Everyone in the gallery of revolutionary personages played his part, great or small, in the revolution's progress. Even though, after 1915, Villa became a simple guerrilla, he nevertheless contributed decisively to undermining some of the key pillars of the old oligarchic order established by Díaz. After the collapse of Huerta in 1914, in fact, the entire state apparatus was dissolved, the federal army disappeared, and the political weight of the landowners was destroyed. Villa was among the principal craftsmen of this social and political upheaval. In 1911, Díaz, his ministers, and the principal power figures in the regime were expelled. While Huerta favored a qualified resurgence of the old dominant class, this short-lived revival rendered all the more

## VILLA'S DEATH

Ramón Puente, doctor and journalist, fought in Villa's ranks. Although he was exiled until 1934, he nevertheless conveyed many observations of the revolution. In a book published in 1938, he describes the death of Villa: "They say that his last words were, 'a hooray for my brothers of race,' as he often called the Mexican people. School children were the first to learn of his death, as the bells rang out at 8 o'clock. A splendid July sun lit the macabre scene; the story, then, reverberated through all of the world's newspapers. Villa was the only revolutionary without frontiers, possibly because of his great humanity and legendary story. The most reluctant to recognize his greatness were many Mexicans, themselves – especially the intellectuals, whose dogmatism blocks their capacity to understand instinct. Officially, he remains an outlaw, to whom no honors and thanks are due. But in the depths of popular sentiment, he was never condemned... and this is his legacy." ■

From: Rámon Puente, *La dictadura, la revolución y sus hombres* (Mexico City: BINEHRM, 1985)

decisive its later fall. The families of the oligarchies survived because, after abandoning the country, they escaped possible recrimination. Although after 1920, many members of the old dominant class returned to power, the elite from the days of Porfirio Díaz were, by then, weakened as an active political group.

With the fall of Huerta, the federal army disappeared as an institution; this is the only example in Latin American history of a professional army defeated by the armed masses. Villa's contribution in this area was one of the most decisive in bringing about change in revolutionary Mexico. If, at a certain point, he welcomed a number of former officers to his movement, this did not subtract from the fact that the army, the most solid support structure of the old social and political order, succumbed under the blows of the División del Norte. With time, a new revolutionary army emerged, which was highly politicized, strongly populist, and for this reason, not very respectful of hierarchies or discipline. In Morelos, ex-combatants of Zapata joined; as at San Luis Potosí and Veracruz, the veterans who fought for agrarian demands became integrated in this new army.

*The old Díaz elite needed only to keep its distance, or else adopt positions moderately aligned with those of post-revolutionary governments, in order to safeguard its economic interests.*

## The Revolution's Legacy

Many protagonists of the revolution governed the country through the 1940s, constantly referring to their own pasts to achieve political legitimization. Governing proceeded, ideally as a continuation of the revolution, as had happened, for example, after 1917, when the constitution was drafted and seemed to direct the life of the nation. In the countryside, in the 1920s, a permanent popular movement formed. It assumed modern organizational forms in its farmers' leagues, which recalled the constitution's dictates in agrarian matters.

Current historic judgment, which focuses on formal changes, suggests that the revolution changed little in the short term, since foreign capital retained its sway in the strategic raw materials sector, the conditions of the peasants didn't improve, the workers' movement suffered limitations, and the new governments displayed centralizing and authoritarian characteristics that were even more pronounced than those brought to an end by the revolution. But the political defeat of the rural oligarchies in 1914–15 constitutes a key element in understanding the foundations of political stability in contemporary Mexico, in contrast to the chronic instability of other Latin American nations.

The occupation of property, the seizing of goods, residences, and homes of the well-to-do, the transfer of buildings to associations and labor unions were not only violent acts, but signs that the old forms of life of the entire nation had been overturned. Popular leaders with little formal education were measured by the government of men and society, and that society acquired a collective memory of a rebellion against the old forms of domination in the countryside.

Villa, over the course of a long decade, administered property, as well as his own form of justice, com-

*A decade of revolution is summarized in* Destruction of the Old Order, *a fresco by José Clemente Orozco in the National Preparatory School of Mexico City.*

manded thousands of men, named and deposed governments, expropriated land, negotiated with diplomats and high-ranking American generals; he fought against them, escaped capture, and began life again as a farmer. His life alone is testament to a social and political reality that radically changed. Eventually, the revolution settled in institutions, but not before Mexico was turned around. The legend of Pancho Villa lives on. It is the legend of the anonymous citizen who helped bring down a closed, class-based regime to build another. And if the citizens in that new society did not always recognize one another, they did, in any case, learn to fight, and in so doing become protagonists of history.

The revolution of 1910–1917 in Mexico is rarely considered in comparative studies of revolutions, primarily because the "great revolutions" contain specific and general aspects that the Mexican case presents less clearly. This explains, in part, why geographic references continue to dominate political-ideological characterizations of the event.

Some commentators have underlined the revolution's social aspects, speaking, therefore, of a popular peasant revolution, putting the accent on the question of land, and opening the door to agrarian reform and the capitalist modernization of the nation. Others have pointed out that the revolution gave birth to a modern state with a mass consensus capable of guiding economic and social development.

Despite the debate over the character and depth of the changes introduced immediately after the revolution, nobody questions that this historic event constituted a milestone in the successful evolution of the country. Above all, it led to the liquidation of a state oligarchy that had been founded on the privileges of the landowning class. In this, Mexico was the only nation of its kind in Latin America. The revolution prepared the country for a political system that opened the door to the autonomous roles of other social classes. And finally, it placed a juridical limit on the actions of foreign capitalists and imperialist powers. These were the features of political life that Mexico brought with it into the post-war 1920s.

■ Anderson, M. *Pancho Villa's Revolution by Headlines.* University of Oklahoma Press, 2000.

■ Arnold, O. *Pancho Villa: The Mexican Centaur.* 1979.

■ Bassols, N. *El Pensamiento político de Alvaro Obregón.* Mexico City: El Caballito, 1976.

■ Benítez, F. *Lázaro Cárdenas y la Revolución Mexicana.* Mexico City: FCE, 1977.

■ Braddy, H. *Cock of the Walk: The Legend of Pancho Villa.* 1955.

■ Brenner, A. and G. Leighton. *The Wind that Swept Mexico: The History of the Mexican Revolution, 1910–1942.* University of Texas Press, 1985.

■ Cumberland, C. C. *Mexican Revolution: Genesis under Madero.* University of Texas Press, 1952.

■ Cumberland, C.C. *Mexican Revolution: The Constitutionalist Years.* University of Texas Press, 1972.

■ Guzmán, M.L. *The Eagle and the Serpent.* Peter Smith Publishers, 1969.

■ Guzmán, M.L. *Obras completas.* Mexico City: Compañia General de Ediciones, 1961.

■ Hall, L.B. *Alvaro Obregón: Power and Revolution in Mexico, 1911–1920.* University of Texas Press, 1981.

■ Hart, J.M. *Anarchism and the Mexican Working Class, 1860–1931.* University of Texas Press, 1978.

■ Katz, F. *The Life and Times of Pancho Villa.* Stanford University Press, 1998.

■ Katz, F. *The Secret War in Mexico: Europe, the United States, and the Mexican Revolution.* University of Chicago Press, 1981.

■ Lansford, William D. *Pancho Villa.* 1965.

■ Machado, M.A. *Centaur of the North: Francisco Villa, the Mexican Revolution, and Northern Mexico.* Arte Publico Press, 1996.

■ Puente, R. *La dictadura, la revolución y sus hombres.* Mexico City: BINEHRM, 1985.

■ Quirk, R.E. *The Mexican Revolution, 1914–1915: The Convention of Aguascalientes.* Indiana University Press, 1960.

■ Reed, J. *Insurgent Mexico.* Simon & Schuster, 1969.

■ Richmond, D.W. *Venustiano Carranza's Nationalist Struggle, 1893–1920.* University of Nebraska Press, 1983.

■ Robles, V.A. *La Convención revolucionaria de Aguascalientes.* Mexico City: BINEHRM, 1979.

■ Ross, S.R. *Francisco Madero: Apostle of Mexican Democracy.* Columbia University Press, 1955.

■ Urquizo, F.L. *Fui soldado di levita, de esos de caballeria.* Mexico City: FCE-SEP, 1984.

■ Wasserman, M. *Capitalists, Caciques and Revolution: The Native Elite and Foreign Enterprise in Chihuahua, Mexico, 1854–1911.* University of North Carolina Press, 1982.

■ Womack, J. *Zapata and the Mexican Revolution.* Knopf, 1969.

# Chronology

**1910** On **June 26**, the presidential elections gave Porfirio Díaz his eighth victory. On **October 5**, from Texas, Francisco I. Madero incited an armed revolt against Díaz with the San Luis Potosí Plan. On **November 20**, the day set for the rebellion, widespread uprisings gained particular visibility in Chihuahua.

**1911** On **February 14**, Madero re-entered Mexico from the US, fighting in the northern part Chihuahua. In **March**, Emiliano Zapata led the revolt in the state of Morelos. On **May 10**, Pascual Orozco and Pancho Villa attacked Ciudad Juárez (in the state of Chihuahua) and forced the military garrison to surrender. On **May 21**, an accord was reached between representatives of Díaz and Madero for the installation of a provisory government whose task was to hold new elections. On **May 25**, Díaz resigned, heading to Veracruz, where he two days later embarked for Europe. Francisco León de la Barra assumed the role of president in the interim. On **November 6**, after winning the elections, Madero was installed as president of the republic. On **November 25**, Zapata launched the Ayala Plan, in which he asked for volunteers to combat the Madero government and fight for the rights of peasant farmers.

**1912** On **March 25**, Pascual Orozco rebelled against Madera in Chihuahua. In **May**, Villa was escorted to the capital and jailed: he successfully escaped at the end of **December**. But months before, on **September 22**, the Casa del Obrero Mundial was born in the capital. The germ of the future labor union movement, it brought together a variety of mutual aid societies.

**1913** On **February 9**, a group of generals attempted a coup d'etat against President Madero. On **February 18**, Madero was arrested and on **February 22** shot, together with his vice president. General Victoriano Huerta, after betraying Madero, entered into an accord with the conspirators, and was named president of the republic. At the beginning of the next month, Huerta had several governors who had been against the coup arrested. On **March 7**, Abraham González, the Maderist governor of Chihuahua, was assassinated. On **March 26**, the governor of Coahuila, Venustiano Carranza, launched the Guadalupe Plan, which started the rebellion against Huerta. On **March 31**, England recognized the Huerta government, while the US government adopted a wait-and-see attitude, deciding only to impose an embargo on arms sales to the contenders. On **September 29**, Villa organized the  , and two days later, occupied the city of Torreón (in the state of Coahuila), which he then abandoned at the beginning of December. On **October 10**, Huerta dissolved the legislature and set up fraudulent elections. On **November 15**, Villa occupied Ciudad Juárez, and

**1913** on **December 3**, forced federal troops to abandon the city of Chihuahua. On **December 8**, he was named governor of the state of Chihuahua.

**1914** On **January 10**, Villa conquered Ojinaga, the last federal stronghold in the Chihuahuan state. On **April 3**, Villa occupied Torreón for the second time. On **April 21**, US Marines disembarked at Veracruz. Between **May 20** and **June 25**, an international conference was held at Niagara Falls, under the auspices of the United States, to remove Huerta from power and design a new provisory government. At Zacatecas on **June 23**, Villa inflicted a decisive defeat on Huerta's army. On **July 8**, Huerta resigned and departed for Europe. On the same day, the Torreón Pact was signed by Villa and Carranza, temporarily guaranteeing the unity of the constitutionalist army. On **July 15**, Francisco Carbajal was designated provisory president, but decided to leave the country on **August 12**. On **August 15**, Obregón entered the capital. In Mexico City on **October 1**, the convention of constitutionalist generals met and decided to transfer to Aguascalientes. Between **October 10** and **November 16**, the convention met and assigned constituent powers. On **November 1**, the Aguascalientes assembly elected interim president Eulalio Gutiérrez. On **November 23**, the marines withdrew from Veracruz, where Carranza, declared a rebel against the convention, installed his own government. On **December 3**, Eulalio Gutiérrez, under Villa's protection, installed himself at Mexico City. On **December 4**, at Xochimilco, south of the capital, Zapata and Villa met. Two days later, the merged armies of these two popular leaders paraded through the streets of the capital.

**1915** On **January 16**, President Eulalio Gutiérrez abandoned the capital and created an autonomous government of his own in the north. Mexico City was administered by representatives of the Aguascalientes Convention. On **January 28**, they abandoned the city because of the military pressures of Obregón's troops. On **February 2**, Villa created in Chihuahua an autonomous government of his own, which administered central and northern Mexico. During this period, the Zapata movement remained at the margins of the civil war between Villa and Carranza. In the state of Morelos, Zapata initiated agrarian reform, distributing land to the indigenous villages, and defending the state's borders militarily, until May 1916. In **April**, Obregón defeated Villa in two battles at Celaya. Then, between **June** and **July**, he defeated him again at León and at Aguascalientes. On **July 11**, the capital passed definitively to the control of Carranza. On **September 28**, Villa was forced to abandon Torreón and retreat to Chihuahua. On **October 19**, the US recognized the provisory government of Venustiano Carranza. In **November**, Villa was defeated in the northern reaches of Sonora. On **December 20**, Villa definitively dissolved his army.

**1916** On **March 9**, Villa attacked the small American city of Columbus, New Mexico. On **March 15**, a US military expedition commanded by General Pershing entered the territory of Chihuahua, in pursuit of Villa; it remained in Mexican territory until February 5, 1917. In **October**, elections were held for the constituent assembly, which opened on **December 1**, at Querétaro.

**1917** On **January 31**, the work of the assembly drew to a close; on **March 11**, Carranza won the presidential election, and on **May 1** assumed office.

**1918** On **May 1**, at Saltillo (the state of Coahuila), the Confederación Regional Obrera de Mexico, a single labor union, formed.

**1919** On **April 10** Zapata was assassinated in an ambush. On **June 1**, Obregón officially announced his candidacy for president.

**1920** On **April 23**, the governor of the state of Sonora, Adolfo de la Huerta, incited armed revolt against Carranza with the Plan of Agua Prieta. On **May 7**, Carranza, isolated in the face of vast domestic opposition, was forced to abandon the capital. On **May 20**, Carranza was assassinated at Tlaxcalantongo (state of Puebla). On **May 24**, Adolfo de la Huerta became interim president. On **July 28**, the new government granted Villa the hacienda of Canutillo (state of Durango) in exchange for his agreement to retire from public life. On **December 1**, Obregón was installed as president, after winning the October 5 elections.

**1923** On **July 20**, Villa was assassinated leaving Parral in his Dodge to witness the baptism of a friend's son.

# Index of names